BEHIND THE SCENES
Benetton Formula 1
RACING TEAM

CHRIS BENNETT with **Oliver Holt**

My path first crossed with Benetton Formula Ltd in 1993. It was then that I produced a small format colour picture book dedicated to the team. This was my first direct experience of Grand Prix motor racing but successfully whetted my appetite for more, consequently I was determined it should not be my last.

Having made many friends with Benetton it was with much pleasure that in conjunction with Studio Editions, an opportunity arose to produce a 'bigger and better' picture-led book dedicated exclusively to the team.

Within, we've tried to take you behind the scenes of Benetton Formula 1, offering a candid, informal and realistic insight into this World Championship winning team. This book is as much about what happens at the factory, garage and pit-lane as the cars on the track, and as much about the mechanics as the drivers. Without the tireless dedication and hard work of the mechanics and support personnel there would be no Benetton Formula.

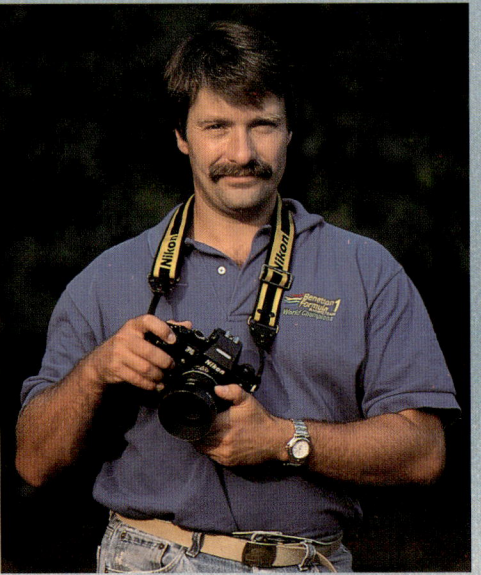

On television the race is all important. The only time we get to see the mechanics is when the cars are lovingly and meticulously checked during final preparation on the grid, and during those brief explosions of activity – the pit-stops.

This book is designed to go some way toward correcting that, and to albeit superficially, fill in some of the gaps. So next time you watch a Grand Prix you'll perhaps have a little more understanding of the tremendous effort required to compete at this highest level of motor racing.

It has been most enjoyable to work with Benetton once again this year and I am particularly grateful to many individuals who made me feel welcome, and on occasions at least, 'part of the team'. I hope very much that these team members who cooperated so readily enjoy the final result of my endeavours and feel that in a small way this book pays adequate tribute to the most effervescent equipe in the pit-lane - Benetton Formula, Class of '95.

Chris Bennett November 1995

Oliver Holt

As well as reporting the 1995 Formula 1 Grand Prix season for *The Times* as their Motor Racing correspondent, Oliver Holt managed to arrange many informal interviews with members of the Benetton team and on occasion even confined himself to his hotel room rather than joining post-race celebrations to get the text for the book written on time. Thanks are due to him for these and other efforts on behalf of the book.

Photograph this page (**INSET**) courtesy Paul Waller
Photographs on pages 82 and 83 (**ABOVE**) courtesy TAG Heuer
All other images reproduced within this volume were shot exclusively with Nikon F4 cameras fitted with Nikkor lenses, principally on Kodak

This edition first published in the United States of America in 1995 by Motorbooks International Publishers & Wholesalers, 729 Prospect Avenue, PO Box 1, Osceola, WI 54020 USA

© Studio Editions 1995

All rights reserved. With the exception of quoting brief passages for the purpose of review no part of this publication may be reproduced without prior written permission from the Publisher.

Motorbooks International is a certified trademark, registered with the United States Patent Office.

The information in this book is true and complete to the best of our knowledge. All recommendations are made without any guarantee on the part of the author or publisher, who also disclaim any liability incurred in connection with the use of this data or specific details.

We recognize that some words, model names and designations, for example, mentioned herein are the property of the trademark holder. We use them for identification purposes only.
This is not an official publication.

Motorbooks International books are also available at discounts in bulk quantity for industrial or sales-promotional use. For details write to Special Sales Manager at the Publisher's address.

Library of Congress Cataloging-in-Publication Data Available.

ISBN 0-7603-0221-9

Printed and bound in Great Britain.

Contents

Foreword 4

Introduction 5

Chapter 1
In Search of Perfection 9
Design • Manufacture • Assembly • Equipment and Clothing • Sponsorship

Chapter 2
Countdown to a Grand Prix 33
Testing: Set-up • Track Testing • Analysis and Adjustments • On the Road

Chapter 3
The Grand Prix Weekend 57
Race Set-up • Qualifying • Fuel • Tyres • Pit-stop • Timing • Scrutineering • The Race

Acknowledgments 96

Foreword

I will look back on the 1995 season with mixed emotions. It brought another year of outstanding successes and Grand Prix wins to the Mild Seven Benetton Renault team, the scale of which we could only have dreamed about when the team was founded in 1986. But it also saw the departure, at the end of the season, of our leading driver, Michael Schumacher.

We fought hard to keep Michael for another year but he felt that at this stage of his career he needed a new challenge and we wish him every happiness with his new team.

We – the 200 staff at the Whiteways Technical Centre in Enstone – now look forward to 1996 and to the challenge of winning with our new drivers Jean Alesi and Gerhard Berger.

Whatever the final destination of the Championship, we have already had a fantastic year. Johnny Herbert repaid our faith in him by winning his home Grand Prix at Silverstone and Michael won the German Grand Prix for the first time. They were proud moments in the team's history. None of this would have been possible without the continued support of the Benetton Family, especially that of Alessandro Benetton, President of Benetton Formula.

I have always made a point of stressing the importance of the role played by every member of our company – from the cleaners through to the technical director – and that is why I am pleased to lend my name to this book. It reflects the effort that goes into producing a winning car and shows the dedication and expertise that is required from all the staff in the Mild Seven Benetton Renault team.

Flavio Briatore
Managing Director, Benetton Formula
Autumn, 1995

Introduction

An era ended at Benetton when Michael Schumacher announced he was to join Ferrari in 1996. He has bestrode the team he joined in 1991 like a colossus, maturing as it matured, growing into a World Champion and a driver acknowledged as the outstanding talent of a new generation of young lions.

In the light of his departure, it would have been easy to turn this book into a prolonged elegy, an attempt to mourn the passing of a golden age just as some might mourn the slow demise of Middle England, the rural England where the new hi-tech Benetton factory has been built.

But although this book is an insider's view of Michael's last season with the team that fashioned him into a champion, it is much more than a sorrowful goodbye. It tells the story of a season, not just of one young man. It emphasises the expertise that goes into the design and assembly of the car at a factory that is held up as a centre of excellence by team sponsors who show their clients round it to impress them. It stresses the dedication and constant analysis and re-examination involved in testing work.

Finally, it underlines that victory in any Grand Prix is achieved with the help of many hands, not just the two that grip the steering wheel. It dissects the process of a pit-stop and highlights the involvement of Renault. It shows technicians and mechanics working late into the night. It is a story as much about long summer days at gruelling tests as it is of glitzy parties in St Tropez and the glamour of Monaco and Buenos Aires.

Benetton is made of many parts and when Jean Alesi and Gerhard Berger join the team in 1996 they will be backed by an infrastructure that ranks with the very best in Formula 1 and a team determined to prove it can succeed without the driver who has been its talisman for so long.

Few will doubt that Benetton is capable of meeting that goal. The team has made enormous strides since it entered Formula 1 as a team owner in 1986 after a period of acting as a sponsor. When Flavio Briatore took over as managing director in 1989, having been seconded from the family's fashion business in the United States, he put a programme of long-term planning into place.

When Briatore spirited Schumacher away from the Jordan team after he had competed in just one race in 1991, the next phase of the team's growth began. Michael won the Belgian Grand Prix the next year and after the team consolidated its progress in 1993, it exploded into the headlines in 1994 when Michael won the Championship, the youngest title winner since Emerson Fittipaldi.

6 • Introduction

Some greeted the team's startling success with ill-grace and its triumphal year was dogged by controversy, by allegations of cheating. It was almost as though the traditionalists did not want to believe that parity with other top teams like Williams, Ferrari and McLaren could be achieved so quickly. The suggestion was that they must have had some unfair advantage.

To understand Benetton, one has to have some grasp of this uneasy relationship with the rest of the Formula 1 paddock. By some, they are still seen as arrivistes, upstarts and posers who didn't get their hands dirty in the lower formulae, who did not serve the proper apprenticeship.

They are certainly brash. Rock music booms from their garage and scantily clad models parade in front of their motor home. Briatore, like his friend, the Grand Prix supremo, Bernie Ecclestone, quickly realised that television was king and is full of radical ideas to improve the show that send the traditionalists running for cover.

But Benetton is a friendly team, too, right up there with Jordan and Mercedes in the common courtesy stakes, well stocked with public relations nouse. Cameras are welcome in the garage, journalists are welcome in the team hospitality area. To a team like McLaren, with its laconic isolationist approach that is only gradually thawing, their arrival must have seemed like a vision of the Grand Prix apocalypse.

And Benetton have stayed true to their philosophy in 1994 despite the tide of controversy that nearly overwhelmed them. The bans, the disqualifications and the refuelling fire at Hockenheim seem to have left them relatively unscarred. They began this year just as they began the last, with a win for Michael in Brazil.

That was another triumph for Benetton's evolutionary powers. It had spent most of winter testing trying to ensure reliability from the coveted Renault engine it had managed to secure at the end of the previous season and performance had been neglected. As the team that had performed the best in 1994, it also was hardest hit by the rule changes introduced by the FIA in 1995.

Engine size was reduced from 3.5 to 3 litres and a stepped bottom of 50mm was added to the 10mm plank that had been introduced in the middle of 1994, to try to further reduce downforce. There were reductions in wing size and wing clearances were changed, also with the intention of lessening downforce. The shape of the cockpit was also altered to improve safety for the driver. The drivers found the cars more fun to drive in 1995, enjoying managing their slides a little rather than feeling they were travelling round on rails.

For Michael, it was business as usual. He won in the first race of the season in Brazil and was then promptly disqualified because of alleged irregularities found in the Elf fuel used by his Benetton. Just over a fortnight later, he was reinstated. Johnny Herbert found adjusting to life in a top team more difficult, especially as Michael had been there for so long and the car was built around him. But he scored points with a fourth place in Argentina and then claimed the first podium of his career with second place in Spain and his first win at the British Grand Prix. Proving the sceptics wrong he repeated this feat with victory at Monza.

But the theme of the season was the duel conducted between Michael and his main rival in 1994, Williams' Damon Hill. They had never been the best of friends but their enmity grew after they collided during the British Grand Prix at Silverstone and then when Hill accused Michael a month later, of dangerous driving during the Belgian Grand Prix. It all made for good box office and there were more staged handshakes for the benefit of the cameras.

Once again, though, Benetton were in there fighting for both Championships, drawing the team around them and shrugging off setbacks. From Briatore's elegant office at Enstone, right down through the company to the shop floor and the test team, the will to win is infused.

1995 was the season in which Michael Schumacher decided to leave for a new challenge. But it was also the year when he faced his biggest test: the task of retaining the drivers' Championship. The preparation for Michael's assault began in the autumn of 1994 in the design room at Enstone: after his thrilling victory in October's European Grand Prix at Nürburgring, Benetton's second consecutive World Championship seemed assured. The foundations for the 1996 challenge of Alesi and Berger have already been laid. This is the story of a team and its drivers.

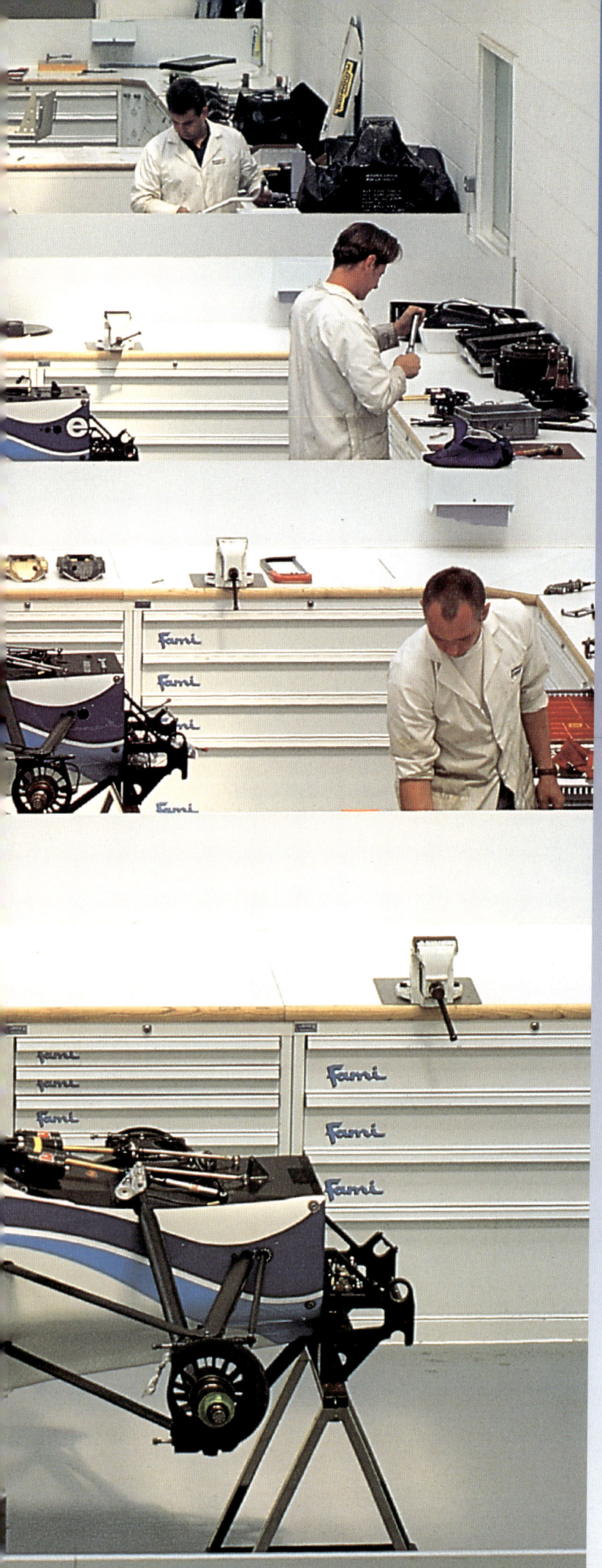

Chapter 1

In Search of Perfection

The quest for speed is crucial in Formula 1 but it is not everything. The car that completes a given number of laps in the quickest time wins the Grand Prix. That is not in question. But speed can be compromised by other factors, sabotaged by failures. It needs to be nurtured.

Ultimately, the quest for speed takes second place to the search for perfection, a search that, as this chapter will show, relies on the most advanced machinery industry can offer. Benetton's ideal is to have every component part of the team working in harmony, working efficiently, reliably, confidently, and quickly.

The search revolves as much around events at Enstone as on the circuits of the world. An hour and a half from London, half an hour from Silverstone, Enstone is a good place for a quest to start – spick and span inside, strikingly modern on the exterior. The first steps are taken in the drawing office, with the first outline sketches of the new car, made at least three months before the close of the previous season.

The search continues with preliminary work on the design and construction of the car – the B195. In 1995, the cars were altered radically because of rule changes introduced by the International Motor Sport Federation (FIA), the sport's governing body. They reduced the amount of downforce, the effect that keeps the cars pinned to the track.

Building for the future: on a factory floor kept spotless by a staff of 11 cleaners who work round the clock, a continuous process of stripping the cars down and then putting them back together is one of the staples of the season. After each Grand Prix, the cars are brought back to Enstone and taken apart. Before each Grand Prix, they are resprayed and reassembled, a task that takes about 36 hours, before being loaded on to the transporters and sent back into battle.

Design

This is the realm of the future, the part of the factory where dreams are made, sketched out with the aid of CAD/CAM, or computer aided design. Hewlett Packard, who supply Benetton with computers, are so proud of the environment in which they are placed that they show potential clients around the factory at Enstone as an example of their latest equipment being used at the cutting edge of industry.

Under the guidance of Benetton's technical director, Ross Brawn, work begins in August or September on the design of the next year's car. Any rule changes introduced by the FIA – and these are often radical – have to be incorporated into the ideas which are sketched out, debated and then sent to the wind tunnel in Farnborough to test their efficiency. Power is not an issue here. The aerodynamics of the car and its constituent parts are the chief area of interest.

As the season progresses, the design department progresses too, working ceaselessly on the development of new parts to be tested by the team, trying to gain an edge over their opponents, keeping their innovations closely guarded secrets.

BELOW Computers are gradually making the use of the traditional drawing board in the design shop redundant but some, like Tony Shrimpton, standing, prefer to make preliminary impressions on paper. The shape of things to come appears first here, in one of four departments under the control of the team's technical director, Ross Brawn.

Design • 11

ABOVE Screen test: one of the principal features of the design shop is the use of the CAD/CAM (computer aided design/manufacture) techniques. In the forefront, a team member analyses the varying effects of simulated stress loads on the structure of the car, aided by his colleague at the next terminal. At the end, another employee programmes manufacturing machines on the factory floor. Benetton use Hewlett Packard computers, Compaq notebook pcs, EDS for the CAD/CAM system, Oracle for database software and Fluent Europe for computational fluid dynamics.

12 • In Search of Perfection

ABOVE Andrew Saunders puts the finishing touches to the design of the model car that Benetton will put into the wind tunnel. Once in the tunnel the model, which is usually a scale replica about one quarter the size of the real thing is buffeted by gusts of air, to assess the effectiveness of the car's aerodynamics. Benetton use a facility in Farnborough, about an hour's drive from Enstone, but are planning to build their own tunnel within the next two years.

RIGHT It may look a little flimsy but the carbon fibre rear wing of a Formula 1 car can withstand downforce pressures of approximately 2,000lbs. On high-downforce tracks like the Hungaroring, the team runs with a lot of rear wing but at low-downforce circuits such as Hockenheim it is much reduced.

Design • 13

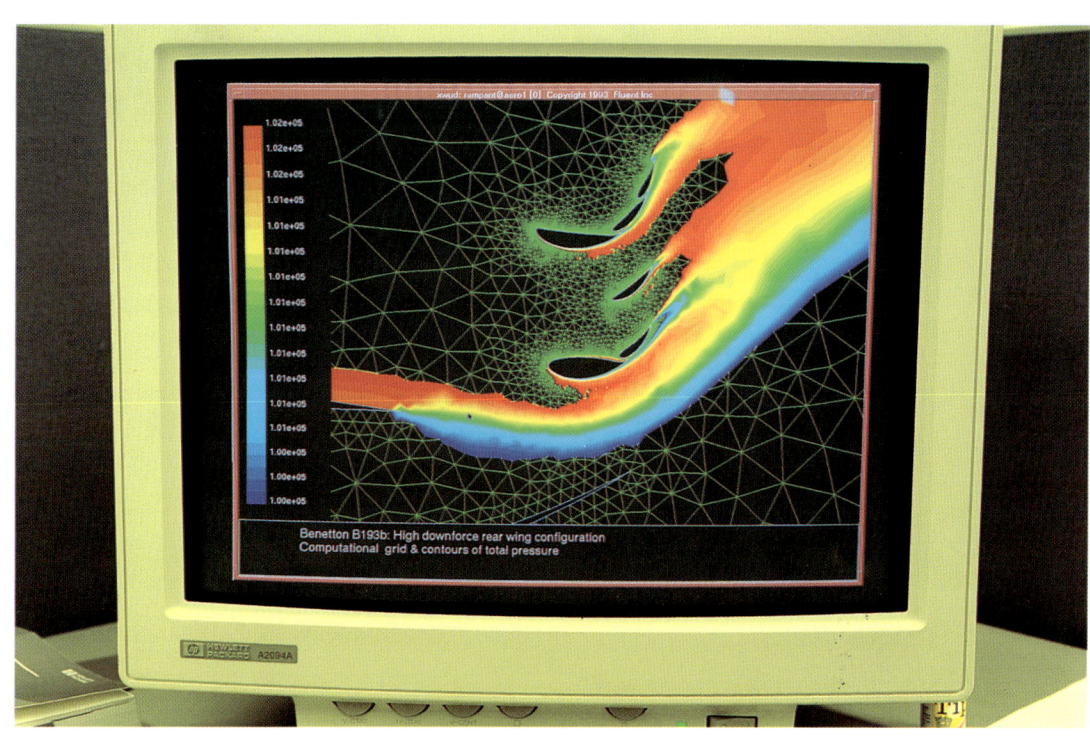

ABOVE 'United Colors of Benetton': a multi-coloured computer graphic showing the flow of air over a high-downforce rear wing configuration. The differing colours show where the pressure forcing itself down on the wing is at its highest and lowest and defines the shapes of the air flowing over it. This type of information is jealously guarded by each team in Formula 1.

Manufacture

In places, the Whiteways Technical Centre at Enstone looks almost like a centre for heavy industry with its autoclaves and a huge cutting device. Elsewhere, precision instruments programmed by computers carve the most complex and intricate shapes from the raw materials. At Enstone, just as at the McLaren factory in Woking or the Williams centre in Didcot, it is obvious that motor racing is a mesmerising mix of hi-tech industry, business and sport.

The most important area of manufacture, particularly now both Benetton and Williams have the same engine and given increased safety concerns, is the car chassis, known as the monocoque. Once its carbon fibre honeycomb has been woven together to conform to the design formulated by Ross Brawn and his 42-strong technical team, it is cooked in the giant autoclave for one to two hours until it has been properly cured.

The monocoque may be the most complex area of manufacture but Benetton pay as much attention to all the other parts. A failure of a part costing a few pence can cause as much damage as a malfunction in something the company has paid hundreds of thousands of pounds to develop. Ninety per cent of the 1995 Benetton cars was fashioned and finished in-house at the continually expanding Benetton factory.

LEFT Patrick Gee mans the drill press in the machine shop. It is digitally controlled and is used in the making of many of the parts for the Benetton cars. The factory has been in operation for just three years, and only a few items, such as steering wheels, which are produced more cost effectively in large batches, are contracted to outside companies.

Manufacture • 15

RIGHT Costing approximately £600,000 ($900,000), the JOBS machine is one of the most important and expensive pieces of equipment at Enstone. Operated by Trevor Kennerson, it is programmed from the computer room and cuts original moulds for the monocoque and pieces of bodywork. It is also known as a 'five access' machine and is at the hub of the preparatory work done on the cars.

LEFT In close up, the precision of the JOBS machine is evident. The myriad of shavings are the remnants of the soft material which is employed to minimise wear to the cutting equipment, whilst also creating a precise three-dimensional form of the designer's model. This combination of high performance engineering and advanced computer technology is essential in the ever-developing world of Formula 1.

16 • In Search of Perfection

ABOVE Paul Roberts, a composite laminator, prepares one half of the monocoque shell before it is cured in the autoclave. A mould is prepared from an original created by the JOBS machine. This mould is lined with carbon fibre fabric, rolls of which can be seen on a table to the right. Paul is vacuum bagging the lined mould. The vacuum bag minimises pressure inside the mould which is essential for creating an extremely strong and stiff web-like material that results after treatment in the highly pressurised autoclave. The process takes place in the 'clean area' at Enstone. Air entering the room is filtered, gowns are worn and an airlock is used to gain entry. Any dust carried into this area could easily contaminate the carbon fibre laminate.

RIGHT Feeling the heat: Colin Watts loads a mould and its carbon fibre filling into the autoclave to harden and make it ready for assimilation on to the car. The machine, a pressurised oven, cooks the parts at temperatures up to 350 degrees Celsius for varying lengths of time depending on the material involved and the use it will be put to. Together with a smaller autoclave and the price of installation, this machine cost £1.2m ($1.8m).

Manufacture • 17

Assembly

Every nut, every bolt is important. When the components are ready to be assembled, every detail of every car is meticulously attended to. One slip, one moment of carelessness, could cause catastrophic retirement during a race and pose a risk to the safety of the driver. On the rare, rare occasions you see a Formula 1 car limping back to the pits with a part of a wing or suspension flapping in the wind, pity the poor assembler.

After a long-haul race, a race, that is, on another continent besides Europe, it takes the mechanics an average of six hours to strip the cars down and pack them into their containers. When the job is done more completely back at headquarters in England it can take up to one and a half days. At Enstone, the process of assembly takes considerably longer: as with most things, Formula 1 cars are rather quicker to destroy than to build.

Assembly starts with the bare monocoque or chassis, a moulded block of carbon fibre, cured in the autoclave. It is the driver's home and his survival cell, a unit capable of withstanding an impact of 50 G and now made even safer by new crash tests introduced by the FIA before the start of the 1995 season.

Gradually, the 'United Colors of Benetton' and their sponsors begin to take shape as panels are slotted on with front and rear suspension, gearbox and engine. The panels are sprayed and the sponsors logos painstakingly stuck on.

The fragile pieces, like the nose cone and the rear wing, are usually the last to be attached to the car. For long haul races these delicate two sections are transported separately to avoid damage.

When the job of assembly is nearing completion, exhaust extractors can be seen snaking their way towards the factory roof as the mechanics run the engine and put the car through some static tests. It is weighed to check its balance and set-up before being loaded on to the transporter to be taken to a nearby track for a 'shakedown'.

This, effectively, is the last stage of assembly, a process similar to scrubbing in the tyres at a race meeting. The car is driven for a couple of laps to make sure there are no basic problems and then it is loaded back into the truck, ready for the Grand Prix. The groundwork has been done, as thoroughly, professionally and innovatively as possible. Now it has to be tested on the track and ultimately in the white-heat of competition.

Assembly • 19

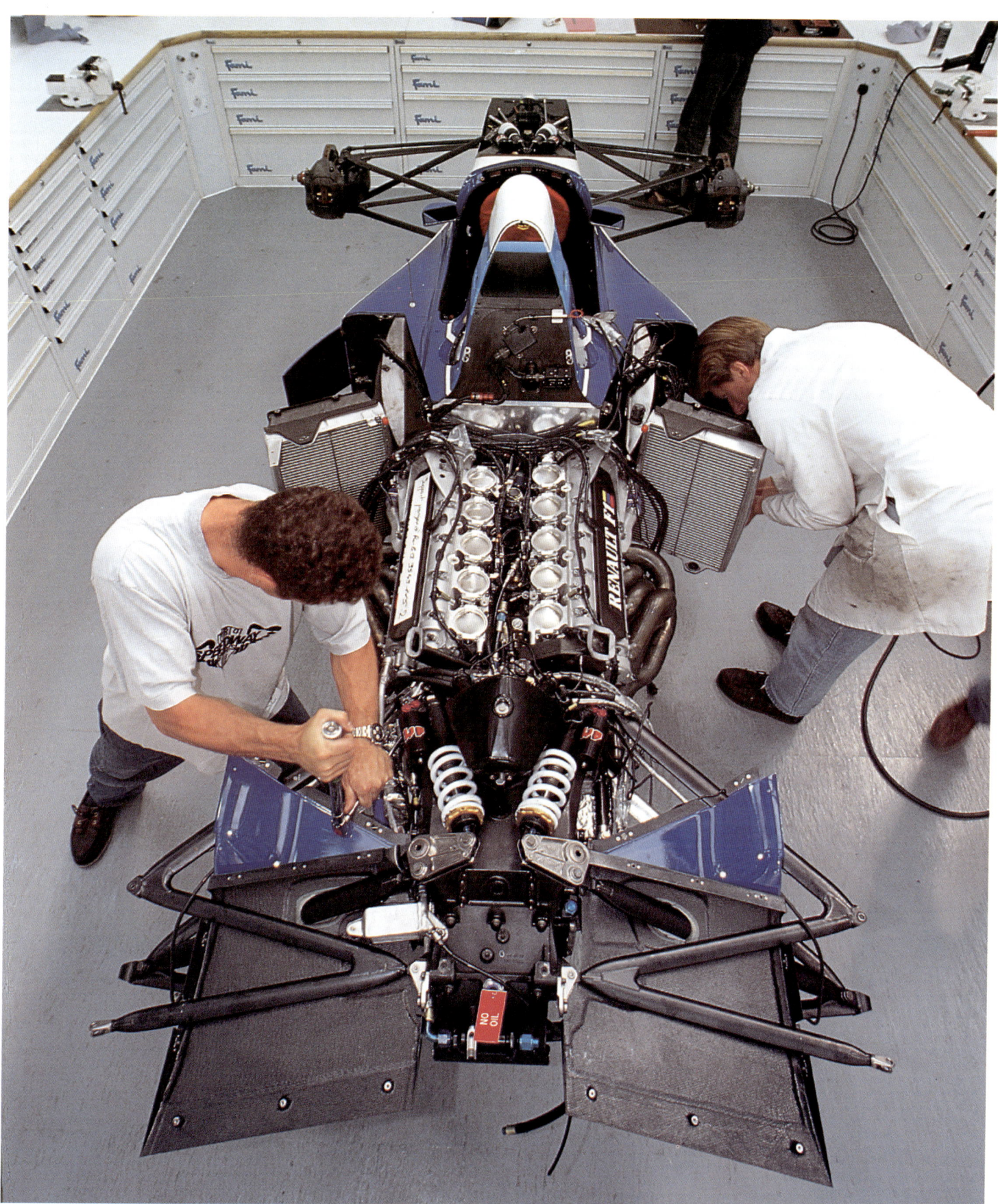

ABOVE Mechanics Kenny Handkammer and Max Fluckiger assemble Michael's car ready for the next race, the Renault V10 engine gleaming at its centre. This one is about 75% complete. Once it is finished it will be taken to a track like Silverstone or Santa Pod, near Milton Keynes, for a 'shakedown' to make sure there are no problems with basic elements like oil-leaks or the dashboard readout before being loaded on to the truck.

20 • In Search of Perfection

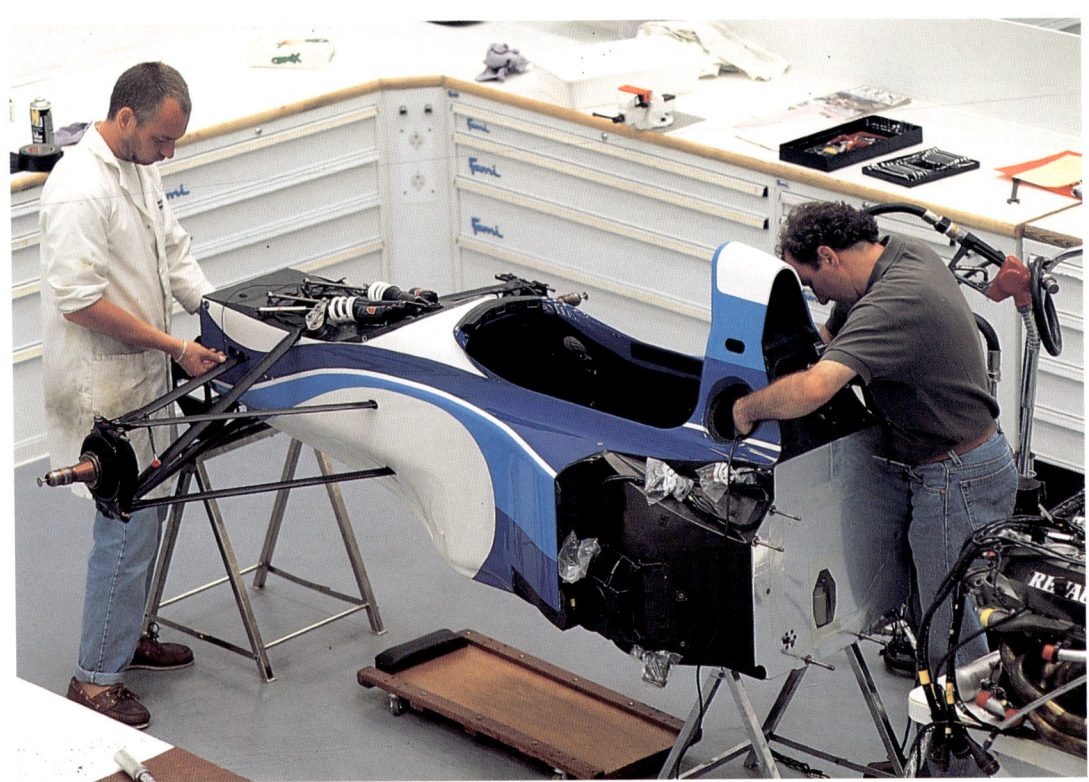

LEFT Lee Calcutt, on the left, and Bob Bushell work on opposite ends of the supported monocoque (known at Benetton as a 'tub'), a prototype of which has to pass a stringent crash test before it is deemed safe to be entered in a race. The engine, one of more than 100 made in 1995 by Renault at their Viry-Chatillon factory on the outskirts of Paris, can just be seen stage right, ready for fitting later.

ABOVE Kenny Handkammer examines a rear half-shaft prior to its installation onto a B195. The mechanics are often asked what they do in all their spare time, when not at the Grands Prix. The truth is that they are all just as busy back at the naturally lit Whiteways Technical Centre. Here after each Grand Prix the cars are stripped down, and all their constituent parts checked for wear and tear. At least one performance enhancing modification is included every time a car is rebuilt.

Assembly • 21

LEFT Hands on: Paul Diggins rebuilds the rear end of a car in the test team bay, fitting the rear suspension onto a spare gearbox. Each of the leading teams in Formula 1 has a team of mechanics and equipment devoted entirely to testing. In that way, the energies and resources of the race team need not be dissipated.

BELOW Tim Baston puts the final touch to the process of putting the Benetton stickers on the rear wing. The stickers are divided into letters and each is carefully cut in half after application. Sticker changing is continuous, largely because of rules banning tobacco advertising at several of the European races. The Mild Seven sticker that usually adorns the rear wing has been replaced here with Benetton, but in Mild Seven's own script, thereby conforming to the strict regulations.

22 • In Search of Perfection

LEFT Protected by his mask, a technician carries out some welding on an exhaust system. The exhaust is made of Inconel, an extremely hard steel, and although it is refined and modified at Enstone, the tube is imported from a company in the United States. Each exhaust costs about £3,500 ($5,500).

BELOW Following assembly of its complicated curves, Max Fluckiger, Michael's number one mechanic, fits an exhaust onto the race engine as the process of assembly approaches the final stages. Swiss born Fluckiger finds the commonality of mother tongue an asset on occasion. Max has a brace of mechanics working with him, although in a structure that is highly hierachical, each in turn answers to the chief mechanic.

Assembly • 23

LEFT On a trolley on the shop floor, it looks innocuous enough, but the Renault V10 RS7 engine is the most coveted in Grand Prix racing. Reduced in size to three litres by the regulation changes at the end of 1994, it is 623mm long, 540mm wide and 420mm tall. It weighs about 132kg (290lb) and its cylinder heads are made of aluminium. After Michael raced with it behind him for the first time in Brazil he was impressed. "I could even overtake the Ferraris on the straight," he said.

LEFT Alan 'Bat' Permane gets to grips with one of the team's aluminium steering wheels. Made by Personal in Italy the high-tech wheels are covered with soft felt so they can be moulded into the hands of the driver for precise grip. Each wheel, with its mechanisms, costs about £3,500 ($5,500).

LEFT The Brembo brake calipers and the carbon fibre discs are some of the most significant parts of a Formula 1 car. Apart from their obvious safety value, the carbon fibre brakes have become so efficient they have reduced braking distances considerably. New recruits to Formula 1 often find themselves losing time to their more experienced rivals because they are not used to the effects of carbon fibre brakes and brake for corners far too early. Their efficacy also reduces overtaking opportunities.

ABOVE Suspended animation: in glorious technicolour, the rear wheel suspension and brake disc sit supported above the factory floor in the assembly stage. Since the outlawing of active suspension at the end of 1993 when ride height was controlled by computers and hydraulics, springs and dampers have been reintroduced to cushion the car around a circuit.

26 • In Search of Perfection

LEFT The car is now in the final stages of assembly, the wings have been fitted and the long hose trailing upwards towards the ceiling is an exhaust extractor to siphon away fumes from the high revving engine. After the 'shakedown' the cars will be loaded into the transporters as they are and unloaded at their destination ready for either the Grand Prix Friday morning practice or one of the Silverstone or other testing sessions that occur throughout the season.

RIGHT The weight of the car is checked by scales placed under each of the four 'dummy' wheel rims in an exercise that gauges the set-up of the car in a static position. The weighing process is carried out on a single flat stone made of granite half a metre deep, providing precise level and stability. The wires are connected to a computer which carries out the measurement. When the driver is sitting in the car, its maximum weight limit is 595kgs (1298lb).

LEFT Part time: Paul Howard picks his way through a drawer of springs to find the correct ones to attach to Johnny's car. Parts for Johnny's car are marked with the number one and the type of spring used varies with the characteristics of the circuit to be visited. Each pair of springs, which are made in the United States, costs £300 ($500).

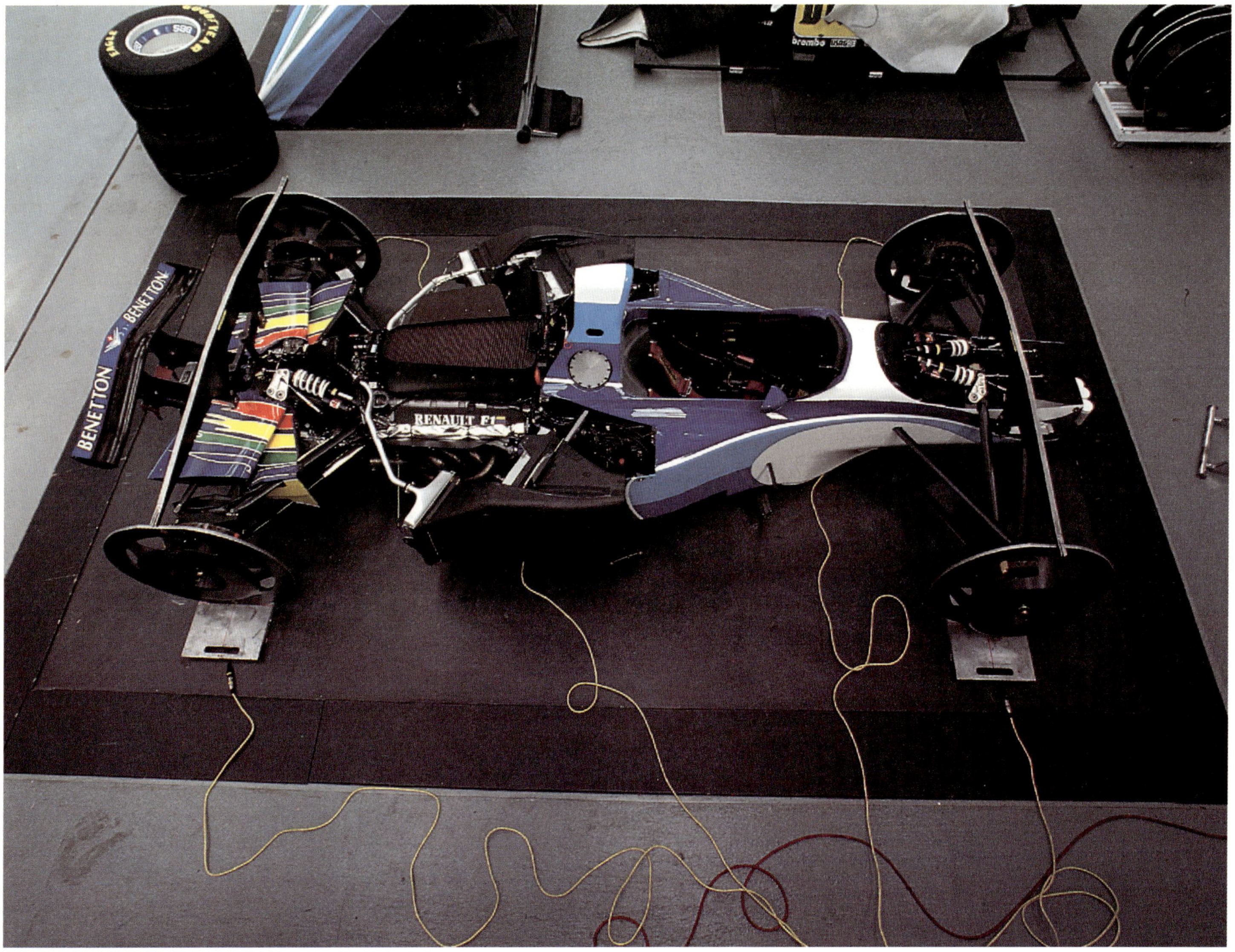

Equipment and Clothing

The paraphernalia associated with Grand Prix racing has increased with the re-introduction of refuelling and the greater concerns for safety following the spate of serious accidents in 1994 which included the death of Ayrton Senna.

Helmets have been strengthened and improved and all the drivers wear fire-proof balaclavas in case their car catches fire out on the circuit or in the pits.

The race-wear of mechanics and team members has also been revolutionized since the beginning of the 1994 season. Refuelling stops have replaced mere tyre changes and the pit-crew now wear masks as well as balaclavas and flame-proof overalls. A brief alarm when Eddie Irvine's Jordan caught fire in the pits at the 1995 Belgian Grand Prix, kept the dangers firmly at the front of everyone's minds. The men holding the refuelling hose must now wear heat resistant helmets on top of their balaclavas.

The pit-lane firemen, with their shiny reflective uniforms have become a useful source of magazine covers and jokes about aliens from outer space. But everyone involved in Formula 1 hopes that will remain the only reason why they attract attention.

ABOVE Members of the Benetton pit crew show off the components of their protective clothing as they wait to be called upon again. Their overalls are fire-resistant and they wear goggles to protect their eyes.

Equipment and Clothing • 29

BELOW Michael checks through a range of helmets laid out in one of the Benetton trucks. He and Ligier's Martin Brundle both wear helmets manufactured by Bell but the majority of drivers use Arai headgear. Jean Alesi and Mika Hakkinen prefer the Shoei brand; they are all heavily padded and incredibly strong.

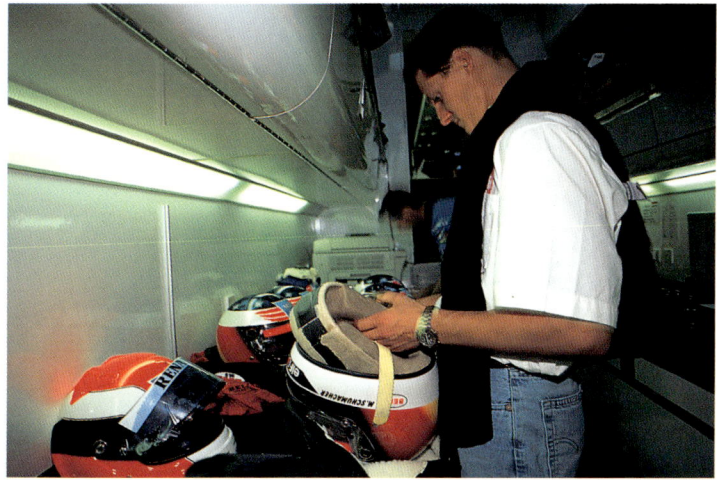

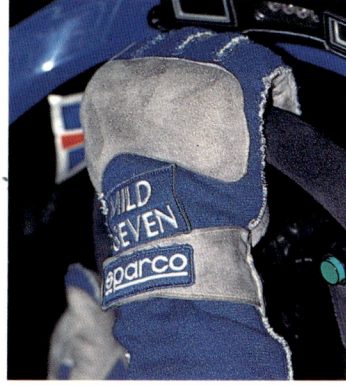

ABOVE Johnny peers through his open visor during a break in the action in the pits. The drivers often paste a series of 'tear offs' on to the front of their visors so that when they become caked in oil or water thrown up by the track or the car in front, they can rip off the detachable plastic strip and move on to another one beneath it.

ABOVE Michael grips the wheel with fire-resistant gloves. The wheel is moulded to the shape of his hands and the gloves prevent chafing.

ABOVE Dual protection: all the drivers wear a flame-resistant balaclava under their helmets. The cable coming from the helmet plugs into the radio so they can communicate with the pits. Michael sometimes wears a heavier helmet for testing to help strengthen his neck muscles.

RIGHT Martin Pople, the man who steadies the refuelling hose as it is forced into the tank, ties on his felt shoes in preparation for the race. He wears a helmet rather than a balaclava because of his proximity to the fuel.

Sponsorship

If television coverage provides the oxygen for Formula 1, sponsorship is its life-blood. Beer and tobacco companies dominate the Benetton cars, stamping their corporate image on their flying forms with bright colours and distinctive logos. They pay, essentially, for television air time, for the camera to linger lovingly on the car they have helped to pay for and, particularly in the last two years, Benetton have delivered handsomely.

A top Formula 1 team needs about £26m ($40m) each season to sustain a serious challenge for the championship, to pay for parts, astronomical running costs, inflationary driver wages and the rest. Mild Seven's deal with Benetton lasts until the end of 1996, at least. They are more than happy with their part of the bargain.

They and other major Formula 1 sponsors like Marlboro and Rothmans are even prepared to accept bans on tobacco advertising that are now enforced in Britain, France, Canada and Germany, which hosted two races in 1995. Other sponsors like Hewlett Packard do not appear on the car at all. They supply the Benetton factory with their latest equipment and use it as a centre of excellence to show their clients. Renault supply the car's engine free of charge.

The three most sought after, and therefore most expensive, areas to sponsor on any car are the engine cover, the rear wing and the sidepods. Bitburger, a German brewing company, have the Benetton sidepods while Mild Seven take the rear wing and engine cover.

Both are also displayed prominently on the drivers' overalls but they have to compete there with personal sponsors. Michael has lucrative endorsements with Dekra, a motoring service centre company, and Omega watches. When he moves to Ferrari, he will be given 'free' overalls which means no sponsors will be imposed on his outfit by the team and he can garner huge sums from selling it to personal sponsors.

Sponsorship • 31

Chapter 2

Countdown to a Grand Prix

So the car is built and ready to trip off the Enstone assembly line, its parts gleaming and its manufacturers proud of their creation. But at this stage, the B195 is still far from ready for the rigours of open competition on the Grand Prix circuits of the world. If the building and assembly process seemed intricate and exhaustive then the black art of testing can at least match it.

There is a saying in Formula 1 that if a car is not quick straight out of the box, you will never be able to make it quick. Each year, many of the teams spend half their winters and a large portion of their season working to disprove the theory, trying to make something that is slow go quickly, trying to coax even more speed out of a car that is already quick.

When the season starts, development work continues on the track and in the wind tunnel, honing and perfecting, listening to the feedback of the drivers and their points about the performance of the cars. Everyone plays a part, from the race engineers to the truckies who take the finished version the final step of the way in their hi-tech transporters. From factory to Grand Prix can seem like a million miles.

Blurring the margins: Michael blasts out of the pits at the beginning of a mid-summer test at Silverstone. The home of the British Grand Prix can be a bleak, chilling place in winter testing but during the warmer months spectators often come to watch. The destination of the World Championship is decided as much by these intensive three or four day stints as during the Grands Prix themselves. The teams try to learn the lessons of the previous race, either building on their advantages or attempting to correct their shortcomings.

Testing: Set-up

From Jerez and Barcelona to Estoril, Silverstone and Paul Ricard, in the south of France, the scene remains the same. In the early morning at Formula 1's favourite testing circuits, the mechanics ease the car on to its stand and begin to prepare it for the evolutionary process ahead, a period of both growth and improvement. Estoril in Portugal, because of its largely sunny weather in the winter, and Silverstone in in England, because of its proximity to most of the teams, are the most commonly used circuits.

Before the 1995 season began, Benetton spent an inordinate amount of time concentrating on ensuring reliability rather than raw speed because of their need to amalgamate the new Renault V10 engine. The team wanted to get testing miles under its belt rather than concentrating on setting fast lap times.

This does not however stop drivers, designers and engineers searching for minute improvements that can shave tenths of a second off a time. Before they go out on the circuit, the car is adjusted to suit the track it will run on. The angle of the rear wing will be altered to provide more or less downforce. Low downforce is required for a circuit like Hockenheim with long, long straights and high speeds; high downforce is needed if the circuit is tight and twisting like the Hungaroring – the closest you can get to a street circuit without actually being on one. Within those basic parameters, the drivers will make tiny adjustments that they think may give them an advantage in a particular corner.

In these days of passive suspension, springs and dampers have to be altered, too, depending on the contours of the circuit and the car's performance over bumps. Each test team mechanic is specifically employed by Benetton and has the responsibility of developing a particular area of the car, be it hydraulics or gearbox, the car's rear or front, and checks it over before Michael or Johnny set out on the track. One mechanic will routinely sit in the cockpit, running through the gearbox once the engine has been started up.

The process of initial set-up is part exorcism of any gremlins that may have escaped detection during the final stages of assembly, and part fine-tuning. The aim is to balance the car as accurately as possible with the benefit of previously accumulated data, but with the disadvantage of never having run the latest car on the circuit and not knowing exactly how it will behave. That can only be discovered once the car leaves the garage. But time spent wisely in initial set-up can save money wasted on lost track time if the team is trying to cure problems once a circuit has officially opened and the cars of the other teams are making progress.

Testing: Set-up • 35

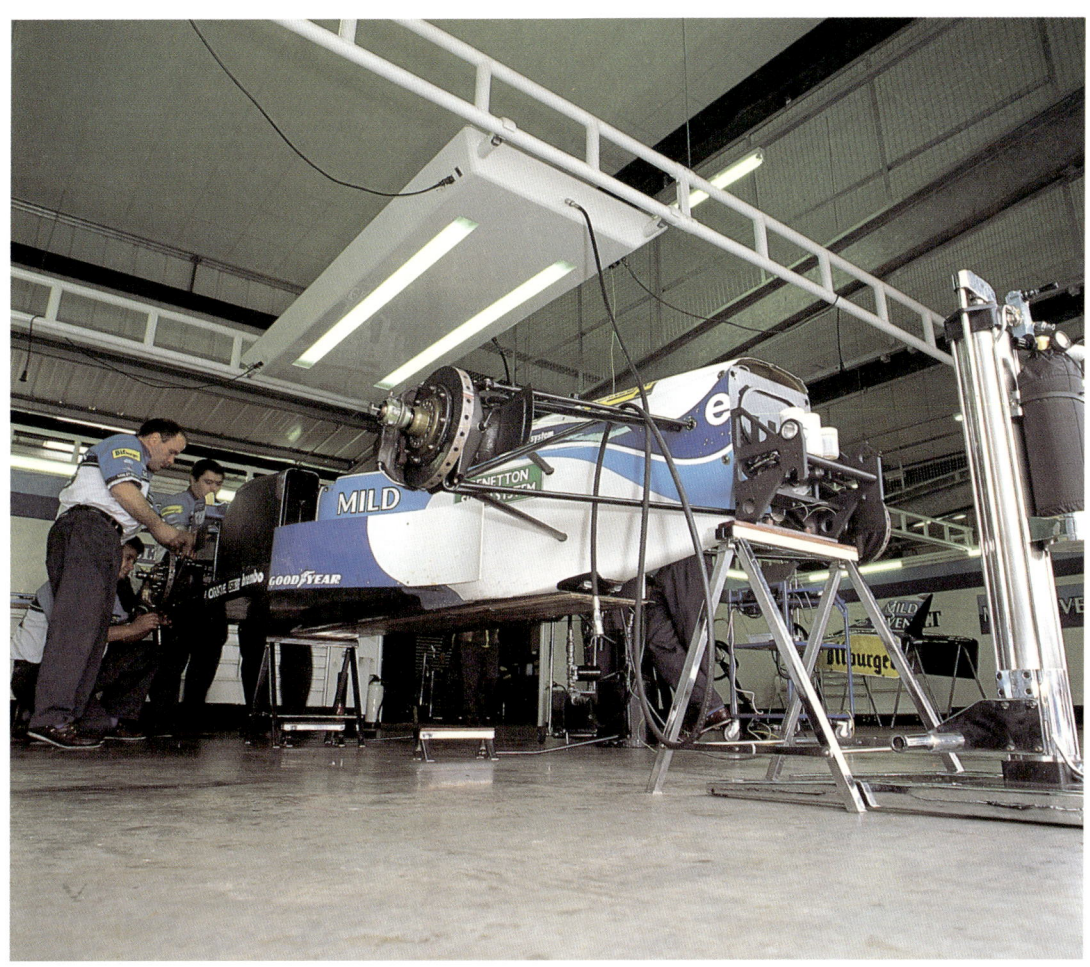

LEFT Michael's Benetton Renault sits on its stands in the garage as the mechanics prepare it for action. An air-jack is placed at the right of the picture. At Silverstone, the track usually opens for testing at 10am and runs through until 1pm, re-opening from 2pm until 5pm. But when the Benetton team tested at Jerez in southern Spain in the spring, they were granted permission to start at 7am and finish earlier because of the intense heat.

LEFT Glyn Beeby, who holds responsibility for the car's hydraulics within the test team, pores over the data logger to study feedback. Around him, other members of the team, all of whom have pre-assigned duties, perform their checks before the driver gets into the car.

36 • Countdown to a Grand Prix

ABOVE Hands on: the test team go to work on adjustments to Michael's car. Glyn Beeby, in the centre is wearing gloves to protect his hands as he makes a small change to the gearbox oil cooler. To his right, Carlos Nunes, the test car's number one mechanic, performs a supporting role and beyond him, Paul Wesson, the gearbox man, looks on. Paul Diggins, at the right of the picture, works on an unseen part of the rear end.

LEFT Food for thought: Michael drinks one of the unappetising concoctions prepared for him by his personal dietician and physical trainer, the Austrian, Harry Hawelka (**ABOVE RIGHT**). A gruel-like soup is in the basin but the ingredients are kept a secret as are all details of Michael's diet. Hawelka travels with Michael to all races and tests to prepare his food for him. Michael is careful with his diet and fanatical about his fitness, but still tries to eat normally away from the track. He will eat a three course meal at a restaurant but usually avoids red meat. At a family barbeque a week before the German Grand Prix, he ate a hamburger and it stopped him training the next day because he had grown so unaccustomed to digesting its ingredients!

Testing: Set-up • 37

BELOW Carlos Nunes, right, and Carl 'Skippy' Gibson, begin to lift the engine cover into place. It is the final piece in the jigsaw, the last part of the bodywork to be slotted on before the tyre warmers are taken off and the car roars out on to the track. The hood is fitted to the car by means of several 'dzus', a quick release type of screw, developed originally during WWII for aircraft use.

38 • Countdown to a Grand Prix

Testing: Set-up • 39

OPPOSITE The function of some of the mass of buttons on the cockpit instrumentation panel remains a closely-guarded secret but the deployment of others is widely known. The black button at the bottom left of the steering wheel is to activate the radio, the yellow button to its right is for the pit-lane speed limiter. The red button on the far right is for the fire extinguisher and the red lever at the bottom left of the wheel is to fire the first ignition. The small screens show, on the right, that the car is in third gear and on the left the hydraulic pressure reading. The screen in the middle shows the car's speed.

LEFT Carl 'Skippy' Gibson, the number two mechanic on the test team car, sits in the cockpit as he and his colleagues work on set-up. The presence of another body in the car helps to re-create the weight of the chassis with the driver in it but he may also be running through the gearbox once the engine has been started. The data logger cables are snaking out of each side of the cockpit, giving feedback about the engine and the chassis.

BELOW Centre of attention: Michael slides down into the cockpit as Skippy, who is responsible for the front end of the car, prepares to help secure his seatbelts. Outside, onlookers who are usually guests of sponsors, take pictures before they have to take evasive action. Testing days are opportunities for the team's sponsors to give their clients a real taste of Formula 1.

Testing: Set-up • 41

LEFT Michael checks his instrumentation panel before he goes out on to the circuit. One of the myriad of buttons will allow him to scroll one of the readouts to a particular area of interest so that it stays locked on it rather than flicking through figures about the performance of a variety of different components. If there is concern about a cooling problem, for instance, he can constantly monitor the situation from the cockpit.

BELOW Carlos Nunes screws together the rear wing and plate, following a change of settings. The profile of the rear wing and the angle can be changed according to the set-up requested by the driver and his engineer. The adjustments are often minute but they can make the crucial difference of a tenth of a second.

LEFT It looks as if the creature from *Alien* has popped out of the front of Johnny's car. But the metal rod, or pilot tube is a device used by the team to monitor the aerodynamic efficiency of the car and the air speed around its various constituent parts. You will never see it at a Grand Prix but Johnny is about to do a lap of Silverstone with it right in his line of sight.

42 • Countdown to a Grand Prix

ABOVE Malcolm Tierney, the test team engineer, oversees the changing of damper settings on Michael's car as he gets ready to go out for his second run. Springs and dampers briefly became anachronisms during the days of active suspension but now they are crucial parts of a passive car. The yellow box is full of spare dampers of different sizes.

RIGHT Strapped in: Michael's belts are checked by a mechanic immediately prior to his exit on to the track. Michael goes out mentally armed with the very latest information from his race engineer, Pat Symonds. Changes will be made after perusal of the data available to try to experiment with ways of improving the car and lowering lap times.

ABOVE The mechanics make the final adjustments before Michael goes out. In the foreground, the nose is screwed on while at the rear of the car final checks are made. The last step is to remove the blankets that cover the tyres. These insulated wrap-arounds heat the tyres so that they have some grip when they first hit the track.

Track Testing

Testing can be a boring, frustrating time for a driver, akin to an actor waiting in his caravan half the day until the director gets to his scene. At one three-day test at Silverstone in the summer of 1995, Michael managed only four laps on the first day because the car was plagued by a series of mechanical problems which refused to be cured quickly. But track testing can also be an immensely rewarding experience, a time when hard work brings tangible rewards, a discipline where real breakthroughs can be made. After a disappointing start to the 1995 season, when it appeared Williams had the whip-hand, Benetton turned things around with astonishing speed after an especially productive test in Jerez between the San Marino and Spanish Grands Prix.

Such was the speed of the volte-face that Damon Hill was promising to "make hay while the sun shines" before the first qualifying session for the Spanish Grand Prix at Barcelona in the middle of May. After Michael had comfortably taken provisional pole position, Hill was more downbeat. "It looks like the party's over," he said. "They seem to have made enormous strides since the last race." After countless hours working on reliability, Benetton had concentrated on performance in that Jerez test and it had worked wonders.

The process of testing continues unabated from its usual starting point about six weeks before the opening race of the season through to the very last race of the year and beyond in the relentless search for perfection. In winter, the circuits can be cold, inhospitable and lonely places, an age away from normal perceptions of the image of Formula 1.

For the drivers, it is a necessary evil. Their attitudes to testing have changed from the days when it was something to be avoided like the plague, something to shovel onto a test driver. The importance of testing today can be seen in the elevation of test drivers such as Damon Hill and David Coulthard to fully-fledged team drivers without the need to gain any top level racing experience.

Now, testing is something all drivers agitate to be involved in so that they can be in tune with the development of the car and grow ever more sensitive to its feel and its every peculiarity. The feedback the drivers provide is crucial to improvement and lap times give reasonably accurate indications of which team is in the ascendancy if they are competing at a test together. In the midst of mini-slump in August, for example, Michael was well adrift of David Coulthard's Williams Renault during testing at Silverstone.

Laps are usually driven in short, sharp bursts if the team is working on a particular problem or feature, or in long stints to test reliability. But here, even more than during a Grand Prix, the driver's input is only part of the equation.

Track Testing • 45

ABOVE Johnny's car becomes a hive of activity as changes are rapidly implemented. Tim Wright, his race engineer, is kneeling to the right while Colin Butler makes an adjustment to the front wing. The process of laps followed by adjustments followed by laps proceeds throughout the day, at the end of which, hopefully, information has been learned and the car is just that little bit quicker.

LEFT Thinking ahead: a pensive Michael Schumacher waits for his car to be made ready during a break in testing. Some drivers abhor the monotony of tests, others, like Alain Prost, thrive on the cerebral aspect of developing the car. Schumacher falls somewhere in between but his consummate professionalism takes him closer to the Frenchman's point of view. At this Silverstone test, he spent many hours waiting to drive as the team battled with a series of mechanical problems.

OVERLEAF Full-speed ahead: Michael in full flight at Silverstone. Seasoned observers often go up to Becketts to watch the cars negotiate the series of high-speed corners and Michael always impresses – smooth and yet obviously giving his all. Throughout summer testing he was always vying with the Williams of Hill and Coulthard to be at the top of the time sheets.

48 • Countdown to a Grand Prix

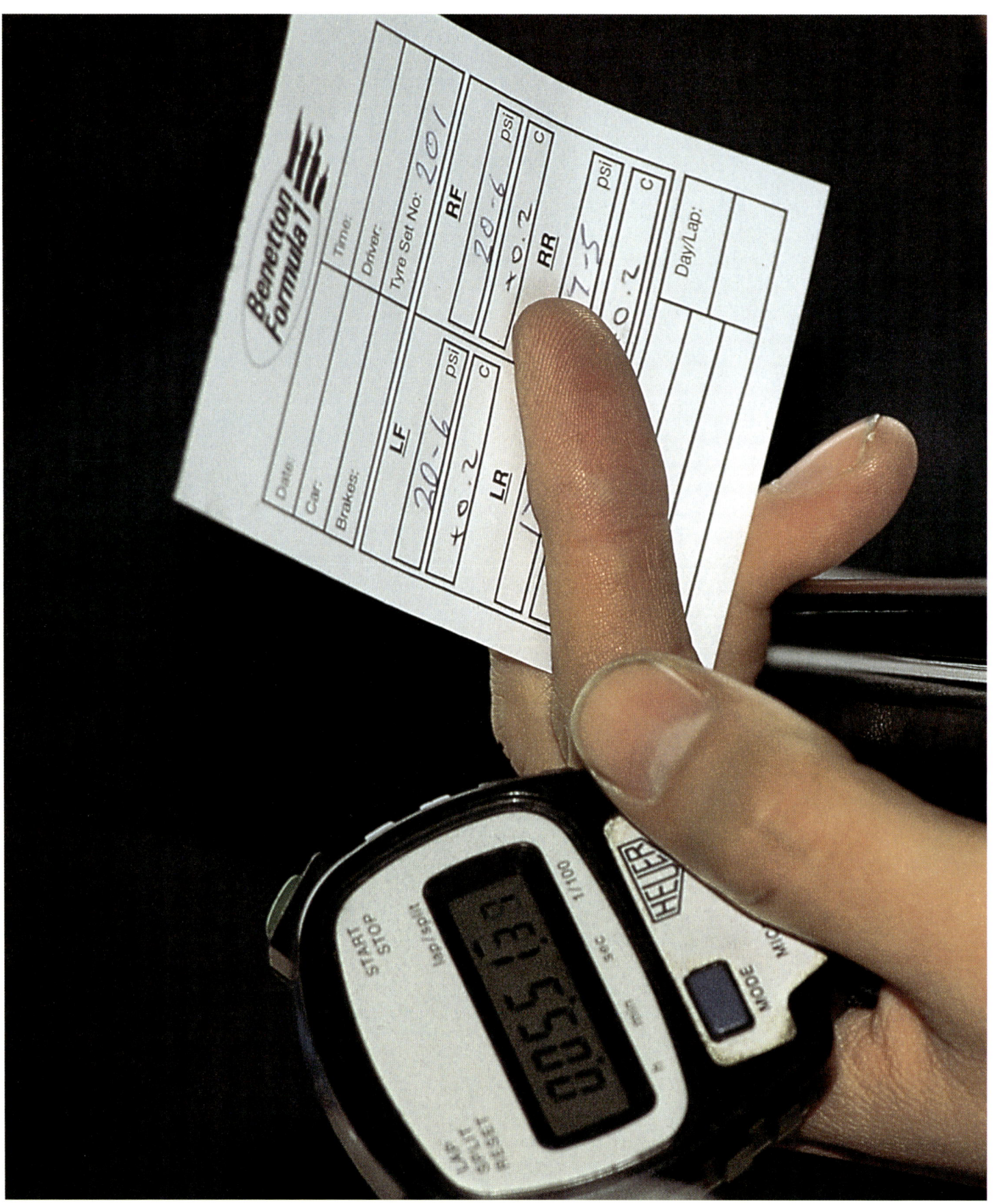

ABOVE A mechanic holds a stop watch together with a note showing the tyre pressures of one of the cars. Tyre pressures are monitored constantly because they are so crucial to the lap times. If they are even slightly over-inflated tyres blister and slide on the surface of the track rather than gripping it. This happened to the Williams driver, David Coulthard, on his first set of tyres during the 1995 Hungarian Grand Prix.

ABOVE Back to base: Michael's car is pushed back into the garage at the end of the day's testing. It is 5pm by now (if the test has not been brought to a premature close) but there is still plenty of work to do. Michael does not usually leave Silverstone until 7pm, after the debrief with his engineer, sometimes cycling back to the team's chosen hotel in Daventry, which is about 15 miles away.

BELOW Dave Coates, one of the test team 'truckies', performs part of his secondary duties. There are four truckies in the test team. One looks after the tyres, checking for leaks and flat spots caused by excessive braking, another makes sure the garage is kept clean, one more looks after the provision of fuel and the last is stationed somewhere out on the circuit operating the team's own speed trap to gauge the velocity of the car at a given point.

Analysis and Adjustments

In testing, analysis of the performance of the car out on the track can be conducted in a slightly more leisurely way than during practice or qualifying for a Grand Prix. Michael or Johnny report their experiences to the test team engineer and they are discussed by a round table that usually includes other mechanics and a representative from Renault.

Pat Symonds, Michael's race engineer, and Tim Wright, the equivalent for Johnny, also often attend tests in order to interpret the feedback from the drivers. When they have been together for some years like Michael and Pat, a driver and race engineer develop an almost telepathic understanding, so that one immediately knows the problem that the other is trying to identify.

After an initial debrief, conclusions are drawn and the mechanics are detailed to make changes, a tweak here and an adjustment there. Telemetry is analysed to sharpen ideas of where improvements could be made by the driver. It is also used to alter the set-up to help the driver manoeuvre the car through a particular part of the circuit more efficiently.

In the middle of the season, each test is usually conducted with a forthcoming race in mind. Before the 1995 Hungarian Grand Prix, Benetton ran a configuration that did not suit Silverstone (where they were testing), but that they were trying to perfect ready for the Budapest race. Setting a quick time around Silverstone was not important – being ready for Hungary was.

The information from each testing run is recorded by a data logger and by the team's own speed trap, situated somewhere out on the circuit and overseen by one of the truckies. Tyres are eagerly perused for signs of wear and tear, fuel is rigorously analysed.

At the end of the day, there is a final debrief, and perhaps an interview with the media for the drivers. Mechanics and drivers often eat their food in an adjoining garage. The preamble is almost over. There is likely to be a shakedown at a nearby circuit and then the cars have to be loaded on to their transporters. But after testing the preparations are all but complete and the shadow-boxers start to strap on their gloves. Benetton are ready to race.

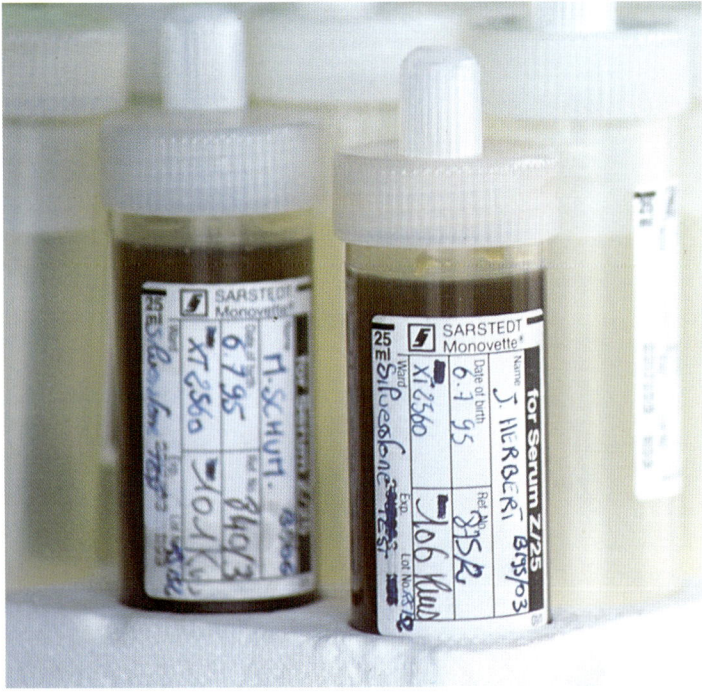

LEFT Oil samples from both cars are put into bottles more normally used by hospitals, hence the wording on the labels. Analysis of the oil, which is carried out by Elf employees, can alert the team to a problem in the car, particularly the gearbox. If the oil shows a superfluity of a particular substance, it can act as an early warning mechanism and signal that there is a malfunction somewhere which may result in a technical failure.

RIGHT Pat Symonds, Michael's race engineer and one of the most high-profile members of the team, studies his driver's Race Practice Run Sheet. On this occasion Michael has driven a full race distance during a test afternoon to try to gauge the car's reliability and its performance with differing fuel loads on board. Symonds is analysing the data that the run has produced.

Analysis and Adjustments • 51

52 • Countdown to a Grand Prix

ABOVE Michael tells Symonds and Malcolm Tierney how he interpreted the car's feel during the run. Symonds does not always accompany him to tests but his presence makes it easier for Michael's comments to be converted into changes. There was much speculation that Michael would try to take his race engineer with him to Ferrari as part of his £40m ($60m) deal with the Italian team but Benetton managed to persuade him to stay.

RIGHT Michael analyses the data produced by the team's own speed trap. It shows speeds at a given point and lap times. In fact, many of the teams use Williams' times instead of the official ones because they use the circuit more than any other team.

Analysis and Adjustments • 53

LEFT Michael listens as Tad Czapski, an electronics engineer, makes a point about the test. The post-test conference, held to the rear of the garage, is also attended by Symonds, Malcolm Tierney, at the top right of the picture, and an engineer from Renault with his trademark yellow collar. Following collation of data from the logger, this select group is analysing it and discussing what can next be tried to improve performance.

BELOW After the debrief that followed the opening run, the mechanics go to work on Michael's car. Each member of the test team carries out their own particular duties. The chief engineer oversees technical changes and the mechanics help Michael adjust his pedals and the seat fitting.

On the Road

For the long-haul races, the races on continents other than Europe, the Benetton cars are packed into containers and taken as freight by plane to their destinations. For the European races, though, they are taken by road, driven for long hours, often through many and varied countries.

Hungary is the one of the longest trips, a solid two-day drive from England. Portugal is a tiring journey, too. Whatever the length of the drive, though, the trucks always seem to arrive in pristine condition, lovingly tended by the 'truckies' who drive them. The Grand Prix teams' transporters, hi-tech and spacious, are the envy of other long-distance lorry drivers but the truckies contribute more to the team than just driving. There are six in the race team, each looking after tyres, refuelling, oil and the cleanliness of the garage.

For all their effort, they have one debit against them. They drive for Benetton all season and never score a single team point.

RIGHT Viewed from the support truck, the two transporters head down through central France towards Monaco for the 1995 Grand Prix. The truckies are famous for the care they lavish upon their vehicles which always look spotless at each race weekend.

BELOW LEFT Ready for the journey: truckies Derek 'Del-Boy' Rogers and, in the foreground, Mark 'Porky' Lee, complete the process of loading the cars into the Renault transporters for the journey to Monaco. The fragile nose-cones are detached and travel separately before being reunited with the car at its destination.

BELOW Resting up: Late in the evening the trucks arrive at a Hotel Ibis in central France where they will stay for the night to break their journey, before an early start once again the next morning.

Chapter 3

The Grand Prix Weekend

For most Grand Prix people, race weekend begins on Thursday when they reach the track. The routine is the same the world over, differing only when races are staged back to back, like the 1995 Pacific and Japanese Grands Prix.

Usually, the mechanics stay at one hotel, drivers and leading team members like Flavio Briatore and Ross Brawn at another. Both groups often work late into the night. It does not take long to discover that the 'holiday' image of Formula 1 is a myth. By the time most people arrive from the airport, the motor homers will be there already, preparing lunch for the arriving team members, a meal that heralds the start of three and a half days of intense activity.

In between is a riot of roaring engines, clicking cameras and spinning wheels. There are morning practice sessions on Friday and Saturday and qualifying sessions in the afternoon where the grid positions are decided. On Sunday morning the drivers take part in a warm-up, then they go into a briefing before they climb aboard vintage cars to be driven around a parade lap.

The race is the climax, but behind the scenes drivers confer with their engineers and mechanics to try to improve their performance. There hardly seems enough time to pack it all in.

Having just lapped a Minardi, and his team mate Johnny Herbert, Michael prepares to blast out of the chicane during the Monaco Grand Prix. The spectacle of the race for victory around the twisting streets is Formula 1's Blue Riband event and every seat in every grandstand is prebooked months before.

Race Set-up

Race weekend is the proving ground, the time when all the hard work and experiments that have been done in testing is supposed to pay off. But Formula 1 is also like shifting sand. Things advance so quickly, improvements are made so fast that the whole process of exploration begins again after first qualifying on Friday afternoon.

Benetton made a habit during 1995 of coming with a late run, falling behind in the early stages of the weekend then working so feverishly on their set-up that by Sunday they were back on level terms and sneaking ahead. Williams often had the advantage in qualifying but the Benetton in race trim was usually superior.

Part of their advantage, in the first half of the season at least, was due to their ability to outperform their rivals in the area of pit-stop strategy, choosing the number of stops that best suited the conditions of the race. But in the end it seemed that Michael's driving could make just about any strategy look good.

The other element in the mix was that Benetton seemed to concentrate almost exclusively on race set-up, working towards getting the car to feel good on Sunday, sometimes at the expense of its performance in qualifying. The result was a car that felt comfortable with slightly more fuel on board and a driver-car combination that left Hill and Coulthard confounded.

LEFT One of the cars is lowered from the truck on the Thursday before the Monaco Grand Prix. The race in Monte Carlo, which usually takes place in the second half of May, is the glamour highlight of the season boasting some lavish Grand Prix functions. The plunging hills and up-market tower blocks dominating the harbour provide superb vantage points from which to watch the race.

RIGHT With the transporter shielding one side and railings holding back the fans on another, the cars sit on their stands with tyres and parts arranged around them. It is Thursday, so the crowds are still thin, but the team has to prepare the cars for scrutineering and wheel them to the pit-lane which, at Monaco, is a journey of about 400 yards rather than a stride out of the garage.

Race Set-up • 59

ABOVE LEFT Michael's car sits in the transporter as Johnny's is eased down to the ground on the ramp. Mechanics from the race team wait patiently to start their work. The paddock in Monaco is the most crowded of the Formula 1 year because it stands in a public area around the harbour that is open to fans. Consequently, it is also the most inconvenient in terms of working conditions.

ABOVE RIGHT The paddock at Imola stretches out in the foreground with the famous Rivazza curve at the top of the picture. To the right are the team transporters lined up beside the pits, to the left the team motor homes and hospitality areas. The motor homes also provide a sanctuary for the drivers when they are not in their cars. At every race, the paddock is home to flocks of journalists and team members, exchanging all the latest Formula 1 gossip.

60 • The Grand Prix Weekend

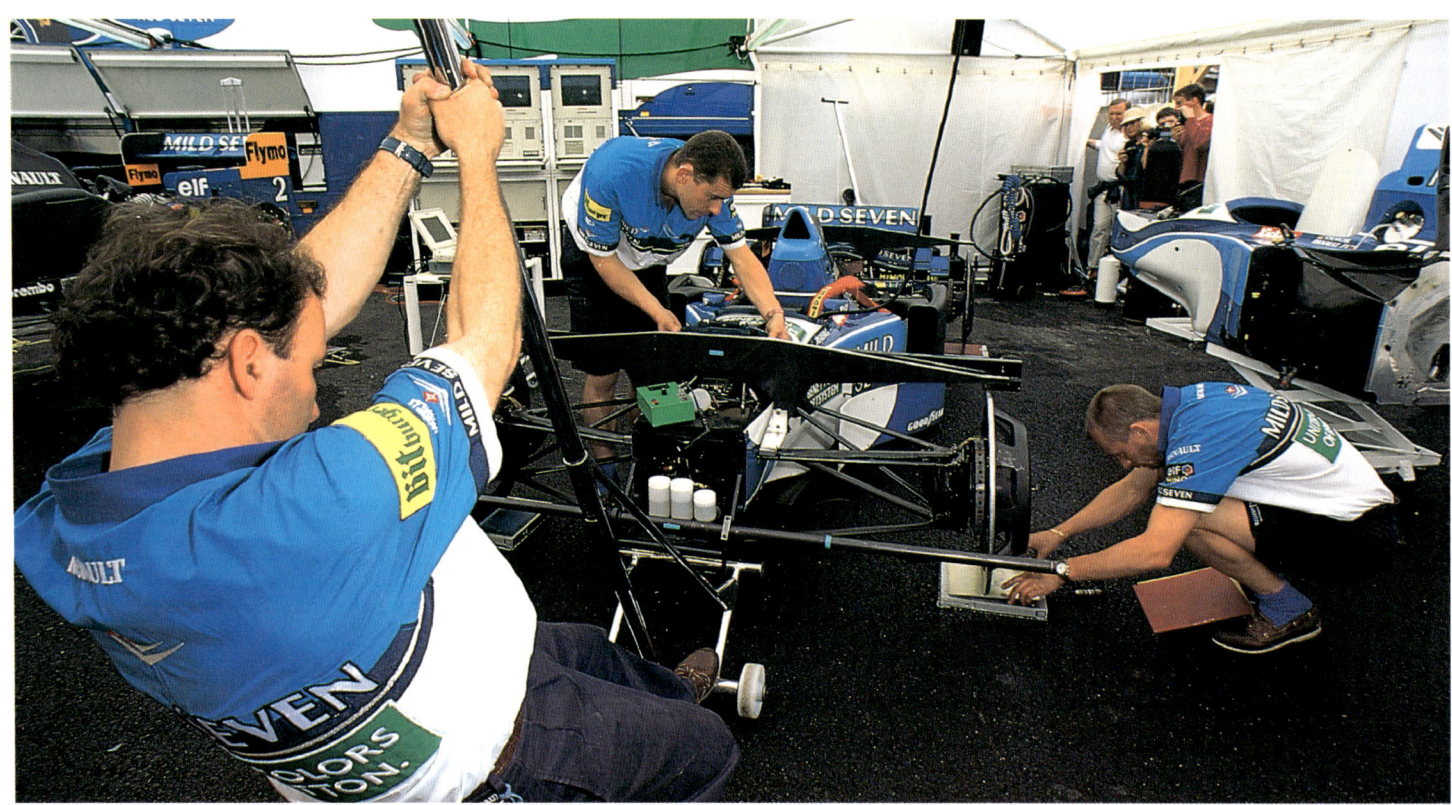

ABOVE Max Fluckiger, Michael's number one mechanic, makes some minute adjustments to the balance of one of the wheels prior to Thursday's scrutineering in Monaco. Most of the team arrive by plane at Nice airport on Thursday morning and are taken by mini-bus on the 40 minute journey to the principality.

ABOVE Conference of Champions: Michael leans against one of the Benetton trucks in the Imola paddock to talk to the former three-times World Champion, Niki Lauda, now a racing consultant for Ferrari. At the same spot and at the same time a year earlier, Ayrton Senna had stood talking to Lauda about the death of Roland Ratzenberger during qualifying for the San Marino Grand Prix. The next day, Senna was himself killed in the race.

Race Set-up • 61

LEFT Bob Bushell jacks up the front of Michael's car as two colleagues begin preliminary work on its set-up and balance. Fans and tourists crowd around the entrance to the giant marquee that is the stage for much of the team's preparation work in Monte Carlo. The pits at this race are so small that much of the work has to be done in the paddock.

RIGHT A relaxed Michael, for once out of his overalls, chats with his mechanics on the Thursday before Monaco. Michael lives only a stone's throw from the paddock, in the exclusive Fontvieille area of Monte Carlo that is also home to David Coulthard and the World 500cc motor cycling Champion, Mick Doohan. Each driver makes a point of having an informal discussion with his mechanics during the more laid-back atmosphere that characterises the day before the first qualifying session.

RIGHT Two of the Renault engineers analyse data on a computer. Surprisingly, Michael's win in Monaco in 1995 brought the French engine manufacturer its first victory in Formula 1's Blue Riband event despite the previous efforts of men such as Alain Prost and Nigel Mansell. It was the perfect way for Benetton and Renault to cement their nascent relationship.

LEFT Michael resorts to brute force as he attempts to alter the metal strap on his watch, as brother Ralf looks on. Ralf is six years younger than the World Champion but is quickly making a name for himself as a promising driver. He drove for the WTS team owned by Michael's manager, Willi Weber, and was one of the front-runners in the 1995 German Formula 3 Championship. He finished a close second in a Formula 3 race that preceded this year's Monaco Grand Prix and is tipped to enter Formula 1 in 1997.

RIGHT Michael is mobbed by fans and autograph-hunters as he tries to make his way from the paddock to the pits at Monaco. Wherever he goes, a crowd is sure to follow, and spending time in Germany is particularly difficult because of his popularity. Even at home in celebrity-packed Monaco his passage is often thwarted by well-meaning enthusiasts.

LEFT Power brokers: Flavio Briatore, left, the managing director of the Mild Seven Benetton Renault team, chats with Alessandro Benetton, the President of Benetton Formula Ltd, centre, and Bernie Ecclestone, the President of the Formula One Constructors' Association and the most powerful man in the sport. Ecclestone helped to orchestrate the deal that spirited Michael away from the Jordan team to Benetton in 1991.

RIGHT Guests and team members relax around the swimming pool of the St Tropez villa owned by Flavio's girlfriend, Nina Stevens. The party was held on the Thursday evening before the Monaco Grand Prix as a thank you to team members for all their efforts. Flavio, who was born near Turin, also has an apartment in Chelsea overlooking the River Thames in London.

LEFT Michael and his then fiancée, Corinna Betsch, enjoy the relaxed, off-duty atmosphere of the St Tropez party while Johnny waits further down the line. Michael and Corinna married in Germany in August and held a party for all his fans on the Thursday before the Belgian Grand Prix at Spa three weeks later.

RIGHT Benetton's technical director, Ross Brawn, the man behind the car, greets the team chef, Luigi Montanini. Luigi, who is famous for his pasta, took over at the Benetton motor home at the start of the 1994 season. Ross has been in charge of his department for some while longer.

64 • The Grand Prix Weekend

ABOVE Mechanics fix the plank, or skidblock, to the car's undertray. The 10mm deep wooden strip was introduced midway through the 1994 season in the aftermath of the deaths of Ratzenberger and Senna to try to reduce downforce and consequently, cornering speeds. If the plank is worn down by more than 10% it becomes illegal and Michael fell foul of this rule at Spa in 1994 when he was disqualified after winning the Belgian Grand Prix. The team claimed the plank had been damaged when he spun midway through the race.

BELOW The focus is very much on Schumacher as he is besieged by the world's media with their cameras, notebooks, sound machines and dictaphones. At tests and race meetings throughout the season, he makes time to give countless interviews and on Saturday afternoons he sits in the team motor home to answer journalists' questions in English and German. The top three in final qualifying are also required to attend an official press conference.

Race Set-up • 65

ABOVE Five race team mechanics enjoy a well-earned breather in the Benetton pit at Monaco. Because of the cramped working conditions Monaco is not high on the mechanics list of favourite circuits – but at least the nightlife offers some sort of compensation. With their late nights and early starts, though, opportunities for carousing are limited.

RIGHT Attached to the side of the nose, this sleek, aerodynamic wing actually houses a miniature TV camera. Other favourite mounting locations include the airbox above the driver's head and the side of the rear wing. Miniature camera technology has revolutionised television coverage and can even help teams analyse performance and pinpoint the causes of accidents.

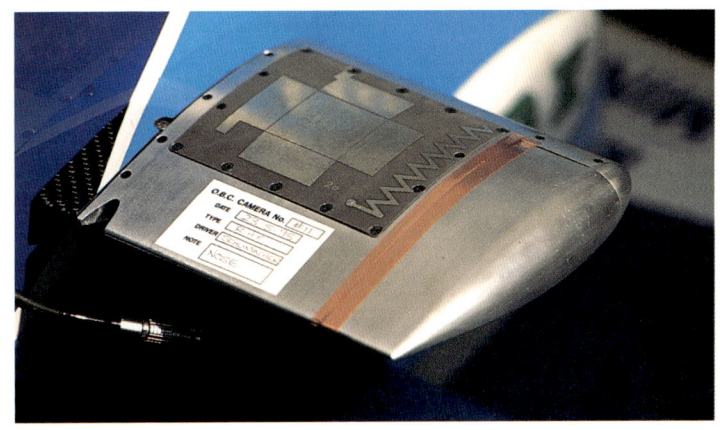

Qualifying

When Michael produced one of the outstanding drives of recent years to come from 16th on the grid to win the 1995 Belgian Grand Prix at Spa, he picked the right circuit on which to qualify badly. Given his own talents and a daring gamble to stay out on slick tyres in a shower, starting from the eighth row of the grid was rectifiable, given the long straights and relatively simple overtaking possibilities. If he had started from sixteenth at Monaco, his race would have been lost before it had begun.

Qualifying is a fascinating adjunct to the race, a necessary preliminary to decide starting position. It is an advantage to be on pole position but failure to secure it is often easily overcome. Its other element is that it provides the clearest guide about the respective merits of teammates and their natural speed over a lap.

Michael's proficiency in qualifying is beyond question as is his ability to perform devastatingly quick laps consistently under race conditions. Schumacher seems to be on the pace from the very moment he goes out on the circuit, never relaxing the pressure on his adversaries.

Working closely, as ever, with Pat Symonds and Ross Brawn, Michael is usually flawless in picking the right time to make his qualifying run. With only twelve laps available, none must be wasted when the track is not at its quickest. Tyres, too must be saved for the race, not used up in the preamble.

ABOVE Michael energetically discusses the qualifying performance of his car with race engineer, Pat Symonds. Symonds is Michael's eyes and ears in the pit-lane while he is out on the track, talking to him over the radio, discussing strategy, the times of other drivers and when would be the optimum time to go for a qualifying run.

LEFT Johnny sits in the cockpit of the No. 2 Benetton at Imola as activity rages around him. He studies the qualifying lap times being set by other drivers on the TAG Heuer monitor suspended in front of him. Johnny concentrates on gauging the track conditions, trying to judge when it would be most advantageous to make his own run. He eventually qualified eighth for the San Marino Grand Prix.

RIGHT Michael is confronted by an image of himself as he flicks through the channels. He usually has a remote control device to change channels but on this occasion he is reaching out to do the job manually. The channels show pictures of various parts of the track and detailed breakdowns of each driver's lap times and his speed through different sections of the circuit.

68 • The Grand Prix Weekend

ABOVE Johnny blasts into the pit-lane to begin a qualifying run. A good qualifying performance is more crucial at some circuits than at others. Anything other than the front two rows more or less rules out a win at tight circuits like Monaco and the Hungaroring, but at power circuits such as Belgium it is possible to score a victory from further behind, as Michael demonstrated so impressively at Spa in 1995.

Qualifying • 69

ABOVE Distinguishable from Johnny from behind only by the design of his helmet, Michael studies more breakdowns of speeds and lap times in the midst of the qualifying session. A few photographers are allowed in the garage and many more cluster around outside, leaping out of the way only at the last moment when the cars roar into the pit-lane.

ABOVE Michael streaks around the circuit in qualifying. Many drivers specialise in setting one blisteringly quick lap but Michael always seems to be on the pace as soon as he goes out. This may be a result of his superior fitness, although that is more important during the race which has been turned into a series of debilitating sprints since the re-introduction of refuelling.

RIGHT Two of the pit-lane crew peer through a wire fence at the back of the pits to get a glimpse of the action. Their earphones allow them to communicate quickly and clearly above the deafening noise of Formula 1 engines and respond with necessary speed to engineering instructions.

70 • The Grand Prix Weekend

ABOVE Quick change: with only minutes of the final qualifying session for the Monaco Grand Prix remaining, Michael leaps from his race car to a spare for a final run. In a thrilling finale, he was edged into second place by a flawless lap from his great rival, Damon Hill, but won the next day's race by a comfortable margin.

BELOW Hidden from view, behind partitions at the back of the garage, Renault engineers analyse qualifying times, adding yet another set of expert opinions to the ones already studying the data. One has responsibility for Michael, one for Johnny, their brief to concentrate on the behaviour of the respective engines.

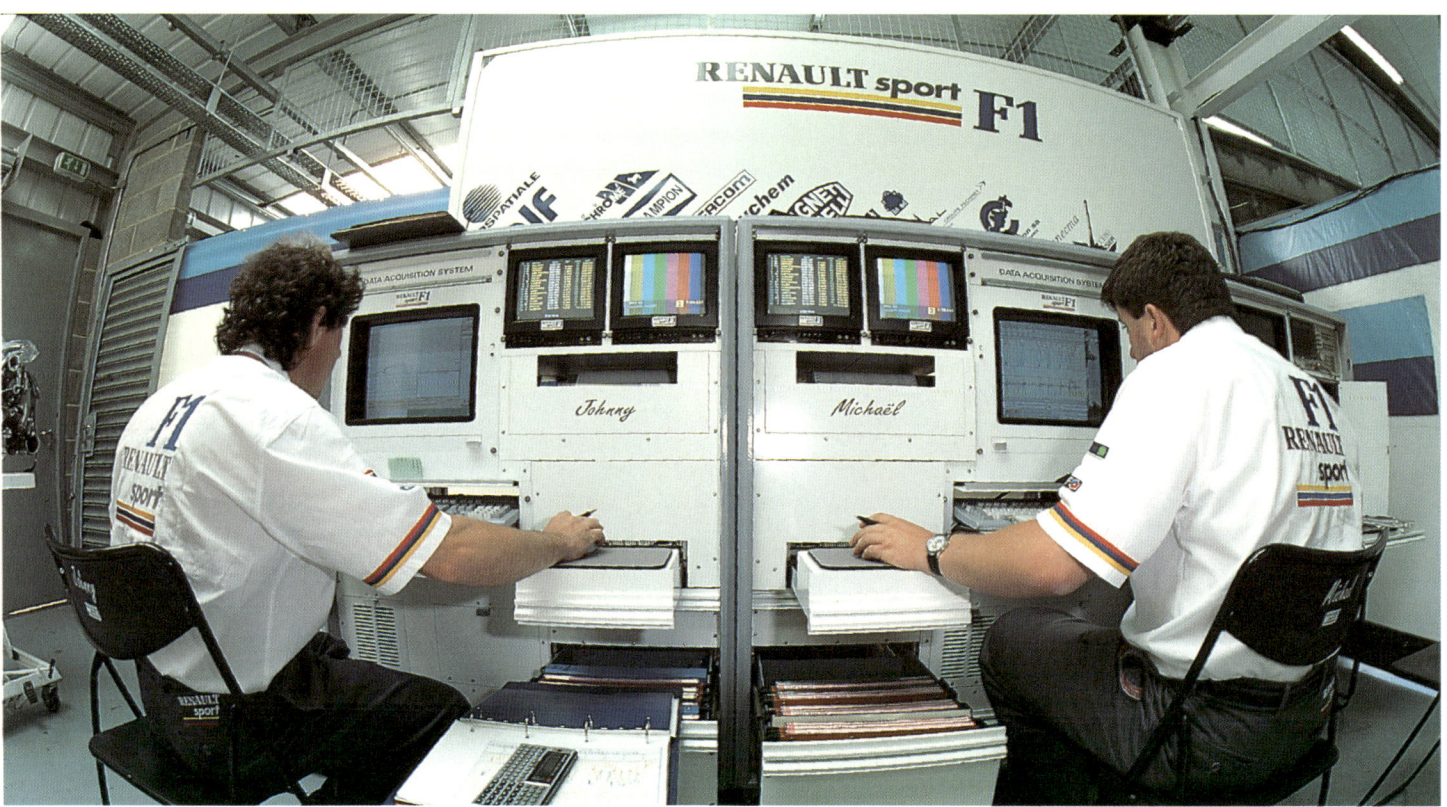

Qualifying • 71

RIGHT Inner sanctum: In the deepest recesses of the transporter, the team takes part in its post-qualifying debrief. Johnny, wearing the white vest on the left, and Michael, third from the right, join their engineers and mechanics to discuss how improvements can be made and how vital fractions of a second can be clawed back.

BELOW Riding high: Pat Symonds sits on a stool on the pit wall as the Friday qualifying session for the San Marino Grand Prix begins in earnest. The pit board shows that Michael holds first place with a time of 1min 29.2secs which he was later to improve by two seconds. He was quickest on both Friday and Saturday but crashed heavily on the tenth lap of the race.

ABOVE After a tough day out on the track, Michael's Benetton Renault has been painstakingly restored to pristine condition and is laid to rest for the night, ready for the race the next day. Michael often leaves the track late on a Saturday night after exhaustive debriefs with his mechanics and engineers.

Fuel

The petrol used by Formula 1 cars has been a closely patrolled commodity since Bernie Ecclestone's Brabham team developed a potent 'rocket fuel' that took Nelson Piquet to the World Championship in 1981. Midway through 1994, as part of the safety drive that followed the death of Ayrton Senna, the FIA decreed that Formula 1 cars should run on a mixture that was essentially pump petrol.

Since then, and particularly since Michael and David Coulthard were disqualified from the Brazilian Grand Prix at the beginning of the 1995 season, the testing of fuel to ascertain its legality has been elevated to a hi-tech art-form, the plaything of the teams and the governing body. The FIA sends its own mobile laboratory to races, now, and the fuel companies have started doing the same.

Even though Michael and David Coulthard were reinstated to their original positions after an inquiry, the affair revealed just what a complex business fuel analysis has become. Each batch has its own 'fingerprint,' that is its own particular characteristics that identify it just as a real fingerprint identifies its owner. The batch tested at the Grands Prix must match exactly the batch submitted to the FIA before the season or else penalties will be awarded.

After the Brazilian Grand Prix, Elf protested vigorously that there had been no mistake on their part and that the FIA had made an error. Even though the governing body did not admit culpability, the commission decided the drivers had gained no advantage. The question of fuel in Formula 1 has become much more than a simple puzzle about how much to put in the tank at various stages of the race.

Fuel • 73

ABOVE The fuel is poured from a bigger container into a smaller one to be weighed before the race. It is then poured into the tank or into the refuelling rig ready to be used at a pit-stop. A truckie is usually assigned to look after fuel in the garage.

LEFT Martin Pople 'strikes a pose' as he feeds the Elf fuel used by Benetton from a small container into the tank. Even the simplest of jobs in Formula 1 is crucial. One of David Coulthard's qualifying runs in Hungary was ruined because his Williams mechanics failed to put sufficient fuel in his car and McLaren were embarrassed earlier in the season when a mechanic misheard an instruction about the amount of fuel he should put in Mika Hakkinen's car, the resultant error leaving him stranded out on the track.

RIGHT Fuel test: Elf carry out exhaustive tests of their fuel and oil batch throughout the race weekend. The 'fingerprint' or composition of each batch must correspond exactly to the fingerprint given to the FIA before the start of the weekend. The governing body has a mobile laboratory to test the fuel and indeed Michael was disqualified from the Brazilian Grand Prix he had won in March, only to be reinstated a fortnight later.

Tyres

After Michael Schumacher had stormed to pole position for the Spanish Grand Prix in Barcelona, David Coulthard, the Williams Renault driver, wandered through the paddock with his engineer and stopped to inspect the pile of tyres by the side of the Benetton truck. He shook his head ruefully; they were almost in virgin condition.

Tyres are one of Grand Prix racing's secret weapons. The difference between a well-preserved tyre and a worn one is the difference between pole position and tenth place. A driver can lose two seconds a lap if one of his four tyres has worn down and lost the heat and therefore the grip to allow him to drive at the maximum possible speed.

At the Grand Prix, the Benetton mechanics carefully clean and inspect each of their driver's allocation of seven sets of tyres per race weekend, picking the smallest of stones and debris from the soft rubber.

The Goodyear Eagle racing tyres, currently the only ones used in Formula 1, provide Benetton's physical contact with the track. They are fitted to BBS magnesium hubs and come in two forms – 'slicks', with smooth surfaces, for use in dry conditions, designed to provide optimum grip, and 'wets', more conventional looking tyres with grooves cut into them, allowing the evacuation of water and preventing aquaplaning.

Both types of tyre come in a range of hardnesses, A, B, C and D, each a different rubber compound. The harder tyres are usually better suited to hot conditions and the softest (D) to cooler temperatures.

They are precision-made to withstand massive cornering and downward forces and drivers take incredible care over trying to preserve them during the race by not running on dirty lines or in dirty air too close to the preceding car.

Even if they have saved one or more sets of tyres for the race itself, the drivers like to drive on them for one or two laps beforehand to 'scrub them in'. The act of running on them cleans off a releasing agent that might otherwise make them oily.

In the Argentine Grand Prix, Schumacher did not have a chance to scrub in one set of tyres. Ironically, because the build-up to the race had been wet, the ones he had scrubbed in picked up bits of sand and dust which were never properly cleaned off and performed inconsistently during the contest. The untouched fourth set behaved perfectly.

Immediately before use, tyres are wrapped in electric blankets set to a temperature of 80 degrees Celsius so that they grip as soon as they are on the track. When the drivers weave around from side to side on the formation lap before the start of the race, it is to try to put heat into their tyres.

Post-performance evaluation of tyre-wear by the Goodyear engineers is carried out in a variety of ways. One is to scrape excess rubber from specific test recesses arranged regularly across a slick's tread.

TYRE DATA - GOODYEAR EAGLES	
Width	Rear 15ins (373mm)
	Front 12.3ins (312mm)
Thickness	0.4ins (10mm)
	(2.5mm of usable tread rubber.)
Average pressure (cold)	12.5psi (front)
	10.5psi (rear)
Average pressure (hot)	20-21psi (front)
	18-19spi (rear)
Optimum running temperature	100-115° C
Cornering force withstood	4-6G
Centrifugal forces on tread	2,500G at 200 mph (320km/h)
Total tyres taken to each Grand Prix	2,000 in a range of four rubber compounds. A-D (hard to soft).

LEFT Michael's car is fitted with 'wet' Goodyear Eagles before the San Marino Grand Prix. 'Wets' look like conventional tyres with grooves cut into them to prevent aquaplaning and to try to siphon surface water away. The tread has to withstand massive centrifugal forces, measured at 2,500G at 200mph. If they puncture, the consequences can be disastrous.

BELOW The intricate patterns of a wet tyre are displayed in plenty in the paddock at Imola. The thicker grooves in the centre of the tyre are designed to flush out as much water as possible and give maximum grip, the smaller, thinner, grooves on either side help to dispel the rain more quickly. Goodyear allows each driver an allocation of four sets of wets over the course of a weekend.

ABOVE Each driver is allocated seven sets of slick or dry tyres per race weekend and the conservation of these can be crucial to how he performs in the Grand Prix and in qualifying. The tyres are monitored constantly and scrubbed and scraped to remove pieces of grit and stone that have become embedded. Here 'Del-Boy' identifies each set with its own code number, whilst fellow truckie 'Yosser' busies himself with pressures.

76 • *The Grand Prix Weekend*

Tyres • 77

ABOVE LEFT The Goodyear workshop, which is usually located at the end of the paddock, is always a hive of activity following each track session. Although there has been speculation that Michelin may compete with them next season, Goodyear had a monopoly on supplying Grand Prix teams in 1995 and brought more than 2,000 tyres, slicks and wets, to each race.

LEFT A Goodyear technician accurately gauges tyre wear, having previously removed excess rubber from the measuring indent. He may also inspect the tyre for damage that may have been caused by heavy braking, which makes the wheels lock up, producing flatspots or worn areas. Worn tyres reduce grip and consequently performance, hence the team's strenuous efforts to conserve their condition.

ABOVE With the help of a computer in the company workshop a Goodyear technician balances a tyre. Any error in balancing would result in the tyre wearing out more quickly than normal. As with every other element of Grand Prix life, this is a precision job that cannot be neglected.

RIGHT The pressure of each tyre is even more critical than the balancing, and is checked with the use of a digital readout. In Hungary in 1995, Michael's qualifying efforts were disrupted because a Goodyear technician made a small mistake and over-inflated one tyre on one of his seven sets. Mistakes were made with David Coulthard's tyre pressures in Hungary, too, and affected his ability to stave off Michael's challenge during the race.

Pit-stop

The pit-stop has become both Formula 1's trump card and its curse. Sometimes the need to enter the pits for fuel ruins an exciting race for the lead, but the thrill of tension it provides, and the skills it brings out in the pit-crews, are undeniable.

Races can be won and lost on the speed of a pit-stop, so much so that when Damon Hill overtook Michael in Argentina in 1995, it was the first time he had managed it out on the track for more than a season. He had beaten Michael several times, but on each occasion his advantage had been secured in the pits.

Benetton, though, have established themselves as masters of the quick stop and strategists supreme. They react to the circumstances of the race and refuse to stick to a pre-ordained plan. Despite the fireball horror their pit-crew went through in Hockenheim in 1994, they have become the most proficient refuellers in the pit-lane.

If Schumacher is the public face of Benetton's success, the choreographed mayhem of the pit drill highlights the team's youthful vigour. Though they dislike refuelling as much as anyone, Benetton have realised faster than the rest the importance of getting it right.

No detail is left untouched in the team's search for that precious extra tenth off their average stop of seven seconds – four and a half for four tyres, the rest for fuel, depending on the load. The wheel nut is machined to fit the gun perfectly, the jacks have special hand release mechanisms, there are safety locks on each wheel. Precise geometric markings in the pit-lane guide Michael to the exact spot for his stop and then the boys go to work.

Pit-stop • 79

ABOVE Dave 'Reg' Jones and Paul 'Seabs' Seaby, the mechanics in charge of the front right wheel, hone their skills in practice early on race morning as Jake crouches, air wrench at the ready. Along with the rest of the 18 strong pit-crew they wear fireproof shirts and trousers during the race; these are virtually identical to those worn by the drivers. Their efforts have a direct bearing on the result and help to turn a disadvantage into victory. Benetton is usually the team to produce the quickest stops.

LEFT Practice stop: watched by journalists and the beady eye of team manager Joan Villadelprat, far right, the team practises a refuelling stop. On the Sunday before the first Grand Prix of the season, Benetton practised 150 stops in the car park at Enstone. Every Thursday before a Grand Prix and every morning of the race they practise another 18 stops. Altogether, they conduct about 1,000 stops a year which may help to explain their supreme proficiency.

RIGHT Kenny Handkammer, the front jack operator, starts to feel the strain. The refuelling stop is still one of the most tense moments of a Grand Prix and the fuel fire that engulfed Jos Verstappen in his Benetton at Hockenheim in 1994 remains vividly in the memory of the race crew although, true professionals to a man, they do not allow their performance to be affected by it.

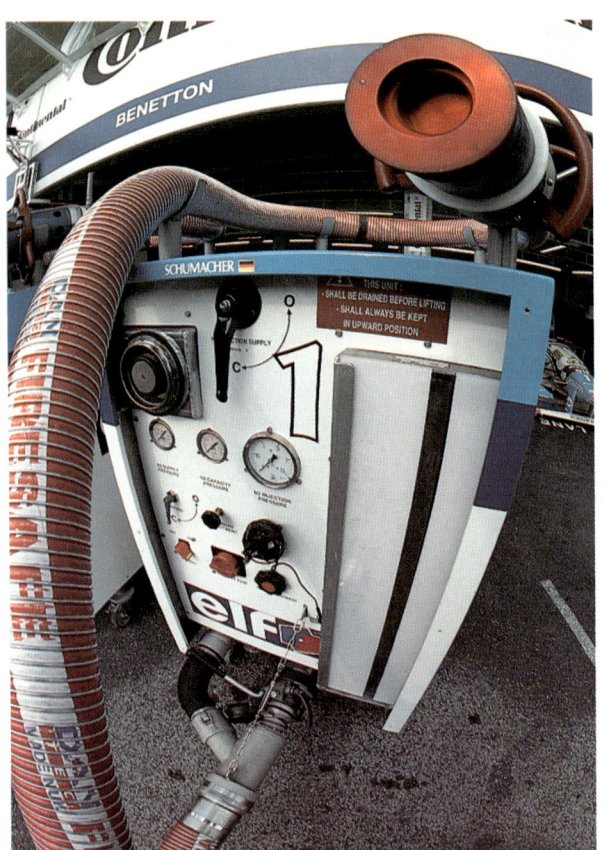

LEFT The refuelling rig that has been the subject of so much controversy since it was re-introduced in 1994.

BELOW LEFT The mechanically operated jack is poised beneath the front wing. Its operator has to have nerves of steel as the car comes hurtling into the pits, stopping only inches from where he is standing.

RIGHT Chief mechanic Mick Ainsley-Cowlishaw examines the business end of an air wrench (seen in detail **FAR RIGHT**), following its use during practice. The pneumatic air wrench, and it's faultless performance, are vital ingredients for a quick stop, allowing removal and replacement of all four wheels in mere seconds.

MAIN PICTURE The full crew: the 18 man team-within-a-team practises another stop. There are two men plus a wheel nut gun man for each tyre. Two men operate the refuelling hose and a Renault engineer is on hand for advice. There is one man for the front jack, one for the rear and finally, 'the lollopop man' who holds out the stick that advises the driver when the stop is complete and he is free to go.

BELOW Steve Bird, the nozzleman, jokes with a colleague. Bird replaced Simon Morley who was injured in the Hockenheim fire.

BOTTOM RIGHT A sticking fuel nozzle here demands the full attention of Joan Villadelprat during a pre-race Imola practice session.

Timing

Without the timing systems that dominate a Grand Prix, the revolution in the television coverage of the sport could not have taken place. TAG Heuer may gain prestige for providing their precise service to Formula 1, using superstars like the late Ayrton Senna to promote their products, but without them or an equivalent, the media would only be able to report the races in a primitive way and the teams could not gauge the progress of the cars. Motor racing as we know it would not be possible.

Timing devices are spread across several points on the circuit, logging the cars as they fly past and recording their times not just over a lap but also over three sections of a lap, showing exactly where some cars are gaining time over others. Average speeds over sections of the track are also flashed up instantaneously during qualifying and the race.

The timing service is perhaps most under scrutiny during the pit-stops. Sensors are placed at the entry and exit to the pit lane and under each team's pit-stop position to give accurate readouts and breakdowns of the various parts of the their stop. The all-encompassing nature of the timing system means there is no escape for anyone. Any mistake, either out on the circuit or in the pits can be seen in the figures flashed up on the screen. There is no hiding place.

ABOVE Jean Campiche, TAG Heuer's chief timing technician sits in the timing centre. The centre is usually located in a small rectangle of buses that includes the FOCA communications unit and Bernie Ecclestone's grey motor home. The banks of screens, which are also provided to the media centre and to the teams, show lap times, speeds over various sections of the circuit, when a car has entered and left the pits and, during the race, the speed of its pit-stop.

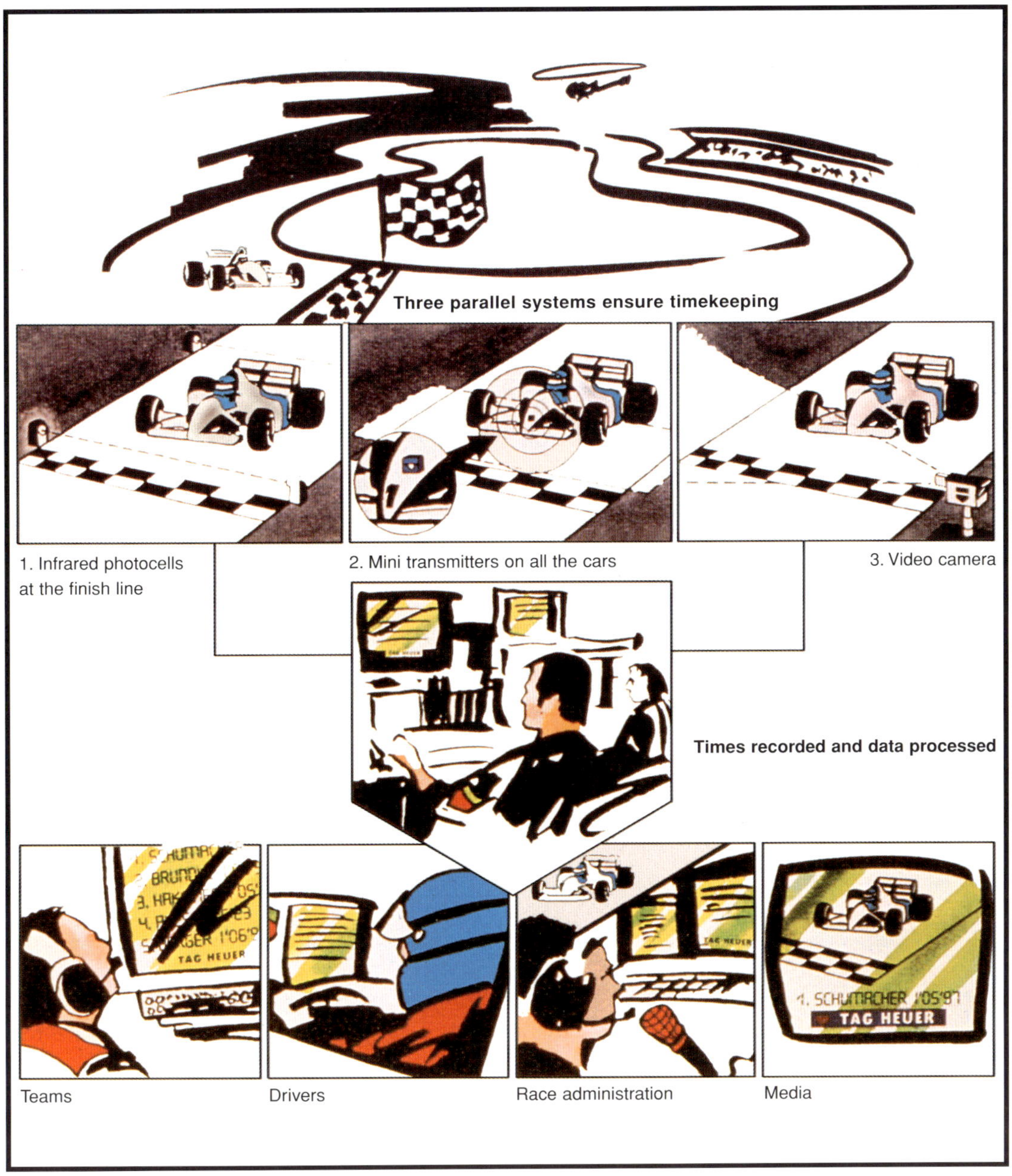

Timing • 83

LEFT A simple diagram shows how the complex TAG Heuer Grand Prix timing system works. Infrared photocells activated by mini-transmitters on all the entrants clock each car as it hurtles across the finishing line. Video cameras record the images and the times are recorded, the data is processed and sent back instantaneously to the Formula 1 customers.

BELOW One of TAG Heuer's advertising slogans was 'Don't Crack Under Pressure', publicised by Ayrton Senna amongst others. If transmitters such as this, placed in the footwell of race cars were to fail, qualifying times – and therefore positions – would be impossible to quantify. Although it might be possible to tell with the naked eye whether one car was gaining on another during the actual Grand Prix, without timing systems much of the excitement would be lost.

BELOW Buried neatly in the tarmac outside Benetton's Garage, this gadget measures the elapsed pit-stop time. The FIA have also now planted tiny monitors under each grid position to ascertain whether cars jump the start or not, a ruse which has caught out a handful of drivers.

Scrutineering

The parade of driverless cars heading for the scrutineering garage at the end of the pit-lane usually begins around Thursday lunchtime before a Grand Prix weekend. There the FIA's technical delegate, Charlie Whiting, and four teams of three local scrutineers, carry out a very thorough and methodical check on every entrant.

He goes through a 44-point safety check on each car, ensuring it is properly constructed, with nothing loose, and that it is totally safe to tackle the circuit. It takes about half an hour to inspect each of the 24 cars.

Each machine is pushed on to a ramp with four sets of scales built into it, flush with the surface, to check that it conforms to the new minimum weight regulation of 595kgs (1,309lbs), including the driver, and that all its dimensions are as they should be. Whiting has each driver's weight on an official list so the driver does not need to be physically present.

Scrutineering has become something of a dirty word for the Benetton Formula 1 team since Michael was disqualified from the Belgian Grand Prix in 1994 because he had controversially fallen foul of the FIA's regulations on the minimum depth of the wooden plank beneath the car. The team was also investigated, along with McLaren and Ferrari, because of suspicions that it was using illegal systems to help with traction. Despite extensive searches that led to claims of a witch-hunt, nothing was ever found.

Scrutineering is no longer confined only to the Thursday afternoon inspection. Gamesmanship began to get out of hand in the 1970s and early 1980s and teams were qualifying faster by running in illegally light cars. One ruse was to replace the plastic seats with samples made out of lead prior to scrutineering!

Now, random tests have been introduced during practice and qualifying sessions. To keep matters fair, a computer chooses one out of every four cars at random and even Whiting has no idea which ones they will be. Rigorous checks ensue to test whether all the dimensions are as they should be.

LEFT Queue jumper: Johnny's Benetton Renault attempts a very low-speed overtaking manoeuvre on one of the Williams Renaults as the sun starts to set on the queue for scrutineering.

Scrutineering • 85

LEFT It's early morning at the Hockenheim circuit and the queue for scrutineering extends way down the pit-lane. The rulings on car design and build are very precise and with so much at stake the discipline of self-scrutineering is of primary importance. As Jonathon Wheatley covers the front of the car against prying cameras, Max Fluckiger and Kenny Handkammer bring out the tape measure for that final quick check. Mechanics often work on the cars into the early hours to attain levels of performance that may gain a crucial tenth of a second on the track.

RIGHT Charlie Whiting, the FIA technical delegate who shot to unwanted prominence in 1994 at the centre of controversy surrounding the legality of Benetton's car, begins his 44-point check on one of the team's entries. Whiting, who used to work for Bernie Ecclestone in the Brabham team, is now based at the FIA's headquarters in Knightsbridge, London.

LEFT Two of the local technical inspectors check that Michael's car complies with the strict letter of the law on the height of the car above the ground. The regulations for 1995 state that all bodywork between the trailing edge of the front tyre and the leading edge of the rear tyre must lie between 50mm and 250mm above the reference plane.

The Race

After all that has gone before, it seems cruel that the efforts of more than 200 people over weeks and months of preparation rest on the outcome of a race that can take no more than an hour and a half and substantially less if the fates are less than kind.

But that is part of the attraction, part of the buzz. Out on the grid in the final minutes before the green light, the adrenalin rush coursing through teams and drivers is tangible. When you stand there amid the throng of mechanics and team bosses, talking earnestly to their drivers who are naturally listening intently, you realise with total clarity what a dangerous and precarious sport this is. Suddenly drivers who have enjoyed a laugh and a joke throughout the race weekend have become deadly serious.

They are, after all, controlling million pound cars in the midst of a charging group of equally determined drivers, all trying to go faster than the next, none wanting to give way. It is a high-risk business where the rewards are considerable but the fall from grace can be as quick as the last race.

But for Benetton, this one and a half hours of frantic action is the raison d'être of their involvement in Formula 1. This is where the real exposure is, this is the time when the most important sponsors' guests watch, champagne glasses in hand, from the rarefied atmosphere of the paddock club. This is when Schumacher struts his stuff on a stage he has made his own.

The races have a habit of providing the most explosive and controversial action, too, be it Michael's spectacular early exit at Imola, his collisions with Hill at Silverstone and Monza or his thrilling dice with the Englishman at the Belgian Grand Prix where he drove the race of his life.

Important though the design, the manufacture, assembly, testing and set-up undoubtedly all are, they have all been tailored to producing a car that can win when the lights turn to green and the engines roar. No amount of excellent preparatory work counts if the results do not come.

But they have continued to come for Benetton, vindicating all the developments that have been maintained and the growth that Flavio Briatore has fostered. Michael won in Brazil and after a blip in Argentina and San Marino, when everyone wrote him and the team off, he blasted back with wins in Spain and Monaco – the most prestigious of all wins and a fine way of sealing Benetton's nascent relationship with Renault who had never before won the sport's Blue Riband event.

Michael won again in France but the icing on the cake, almost the ultimate accolade for the team, came in the next two races. Johnny secured a fairy-tale debut win at his home Grand Prix at Silverstone and then a fortnight later, Michael became the first German to win his home Grand Prix with a comfortable victory at Hockenheim. When the going got tough, Benetton started winning.

The Race • 87

ABOVE At each race, the team chalks up a list of the crucial times to be observed each day. This is race day at Silverstone. Roast Bif is a reference to the French nickname for the English so it seems this notice has been compiled by one of the Renault engineers. The real hub of activity comes in the run-up to the race when the pit-lane opens and the cars stream on to the grid.

ABOVE With flameproofs already donned, 'Del-Boy' Rogers wraps Michael's race tyres snugly into their electrically heated blankets designed to warm the tyres and ensure an immediate measure of grip. At full operational temperatures the tyre surfaces feel sticky to the touch.

LEFT Fifteen minutes and counting: the Imola grid is thronged with journalists and team members as Michael, on pole position, gets some last minute tactical advice from Ross Brawn and Pat Symonds. This is the place and the time where the true excitement of a Grand Prix is at its height, where you can reach out and touch the adrenalin and the sense of danger that goes with the thrill of Formula 1.

88 • The Grand Prix Weekend

LEFT A Renault engineer pours a batch of dry ice down a chute to cool the radiators on Michael's car as it sits on the grid at Silverstone. It is forbidden to pour water on any part of the car on the grid and, with the radiators in danger of overheating while the car is stationary, the intensely cold air given off by the dry ice helps to prevent the problem occurring.

BELOW LEFT Michael, helmet on, puts on his gloves and prepares to get into the car as he talks with Pat Symonds before the British Grand Prix. In the background, Flavio Briatore strides towards the front of the car. Michael qualified in second position for the race behind Damon Hill but the two crashed in controversial circumstances on the 45th lap. Neither could continue, but Johnny claimed home glory for Benetton. The events were repeated almost exactly at Monza in September.

RIGHT Michael prepares to fix his steering wheel into the cockpit on the grid at Imola. The cockpit opening is so cramped that the wheel has to be attached after the driver has squeezed into it. Michael, who was starting from pole position, had just joined the other drivers at the front of the grid to join in a minute's silence for the late Ayrton Senna.

BELOW In pursuit: Michael chases Damon Hill's Williams Renault down the incline from Casino Square toward the Mirabeau corner on the first lap of the Monaco Grand Prix. On the right is the Tip Top bar where drivers like Graham Hill, Damon's father, used to go for a drink in the old days when Formula 1 did not place such a premium on fitness and was more relaxed. Gerhard Berger is now about the only driver who ventures there.

90 • The Grand Prix Weekend

ABOVE Michael triumphantly leads the German Grand Prix at Hockenheim in front of a stadium packed with more than 100,000 fans. Again, he qualified in second place behind Hill but when his rival spun off at the start of the second lap, he was never challenged again. His first victory on home soil sent Michael's supporters home deliriously happy and left him with a commanding lead in the championship.

BELOW Michael climbs from his stricken car at Silverstone after Hill's Williams Renault, on the right of the picture, had collided with him at Priory on the 45th lap of the British Grand Prix. The German was leading the race and most impartial observers felt Hill had been a little over ambitious. But afterwards both drivers were severely reprimanded by the stewards and warned as to their future conduct.

RIGHT 'Lollipop man', and chief mechanic Mick Ainsley-Cowlishaw together with Dave Hughes concentrate on the monitor as Johnny approaches the chequered flag at Silverstone for his first Grand Prix win. Their job is done, and all that remains is the celebrations and then the onerous task of packing up the equipment.

LEFT The damaged side pod of Michael's car displays a tell-tale black mark delivered from Hill's front right tyre after the shunt by the Williams driver's Renault at Silverstone. Hill hit Michael amidships when he tried to dive inside him at Priory. The impact lifted Hill's car off the road and forced both of them into the gravel trap and retirement. Michael and team boss Flavio Briatore condemned Hill's manoeuvre after the race, while the feud between the two drivers hit new heights.

92 • The Grand Prix Weekend

RIGHT A pit-lane fireman, looking more like a being from another planet, stands at the ready during the Monaco Grand Prix. After the burns sustained by some of the Benetton crew around their eyes at Hockenheim in 1994 when Jos Verstappen's car was engulfed in flames, the necessity of wearing masks as well as flameproof overalls was plain for all to see.

BELOW RIGHT Johnny hurtles down the main straight at Silverstone as the team, with Ross Brawn in the centre, watches from the pit-wall. From under the awning, the group react to the circumstances thrown up by the race and decide if they need to change the strategy they had planned before the start. Benetton have consistently outwitted their opponents since refuelling was reintroduced.

BELOW Having powered from Mirabeau, Michael stands on the brakes, decelerating violently to (by Formula 1 standards) crawl around the ultra-tight Leouws hairpin at Monaco. Although the race is probably the most spectacular and glamorous of the Formula 1 calendar, it is also the slowest because of the tight, twisting nature of the circuit. Victory there is regarded as confirmation of leading driver status and Michael has won it two years in succession now.

ABOVE Michael blasts down the main straight at Imola as a mechanic holds out the pit board showing he is in first place with seven laps gone, 3.9secs ahead of David Coulthard and 5.5secs ahead of Damon Hill. Coulthard's board, topped by the Scottish flag, shows he is second with 56 laps to go. Michael crashed out of the race three laps later and Coulthard spun leaving Hill to inherit victory.

BELOW The beauty of the twisty, hilly street circuit around the principality offers some of the closest and most unusual views of the cars. The colourfull, sponsor-liveried upper flanks of Michael's car are shown off to full advantage as he prepares to steer left into the Monaco chicane.

94 • The Grand Prix Weekend

ABOVE The day is done and the fans on the hillsides below the royal palace in Monaco begin to melt away. After the race, the leading cars are locked in the *parc fermé*, a segregated area in the pits, so that they can once again be checked to ensure that they are still within the rules and have not been tampered with at pit-stop. Only then are they released to the team.

LEFT Johnny stands beside the British Grand Prix trophy after winning his first Formula 1 race at the 71st time of asking. It was a difficult season for the chirpy Englishman, who laboured in Schumacher's shadow, but rarely has a win been more popular than his at Silverstone. "It's a great feeling and now I want more," he said at the post-race concert hosted by Eddie Jordan; his wish came true two months later at the Italian Grand Prix.

RIGHT Victory joy: flanked by David Coulthard and Gerhard Berger, the effervescant Michael Schumacher punches the air in characteristic fashion after his historic win in the German Grand Prix. He became the first German to win his home Grand Prix since the inception of the modern World Drivers' Championship. "It is an absolutely amazing feeling," he said. "I can't quite believe that it has happened."

LEFT Flavio Briatore and Ross Brawn, the two men most responsible for fashioning the success enjoyed by Michael and Benetton, toast the World Champion's win at Hockenheim. Some feared that Michael might try to take Brawn with him to Ferrari but he and Pat Symonds have decided to stay and help the team's new effort, spearheaded by Jean Alesi and his ex-Ferrari stablemate Gerhard Berger.

RIGHT A legion of hands push tickets, T-shirts, notepads, pictures and key rings, indeed anything that will accept a signature, through the gaps in a wire fence behind the motor homes at Hockenheim. He signed a rather more expensive piece of paper about a month later, guaranteeing him close to £40m ($60m) for driving for two years with Ferrari and trying to help them win the World Championship that has so long eluded them.

Acknowledgments

Due to lack of space within this volume it would be impossible to credit everyone I met during my exploits. However I feel it only right to name those who had to patiently endure my presence longest. If I have omitted anyone then please forgive my oversight.

I would like to thank Flavio Briatore, Michael Schumacher, Johnny Herbert, Ross Brawn (Technical Director), Joan Villadelprat (Operations Director), Pat Symonds (Engineer, Schumacher), Tim Wright (Engineer, Herbert), Greg Field (Team Coordinator), Christian Silk (Data Acquisition Engineer) and Tad Czapski (Electronics Engineer). Also race team personnel consisting of Mick Ainsley-Cowlishaw (Chief Mechanic), Max Fluckiger, Kenny Handkammer and Jonathon Wheatley (Mechanics, Schumacher car), Paul Howard, Paul 'Seabs' Seaby and Steve Matchett (Mechanics, Herbert car), Bob Bushell, Ray Beasley and Lee 'Lips' Calcutt (Mechanics, spare car). Also Claudio 'Chico' Corradini and Michael 'Jake/Toots' Jakeman (Gearbox Mechanics), Wayne Bennett, Alan 'Bat' Permane and Dave Ashton (Electronics), Tim Baston and Dave 'Reg' Jones (Fabrication/Stickers), Andrew 'Oz' Alsworth (Spares), Simon Morley (Hydraulics), plus of course Derek 'Del-Boy' Rogers, David 'Leady' Leadbeater, Dave 'Yosser' Hughes, Mark 'Porky' Lee, Martin Pople, and Steve 'Scribes' Bird collectively responsible for the three race team trucks together with race tyres, fuel etc. Also test team personnel consisting of Malcolm Tierney (Engineer), Mark Owen (Chief Mechanic), Pete Aldridge, Carlos Nunes, Colin Hale and Carl 'Skippy' Gibson (Mechanics), Colin Butler (Fabrication), Andrew Cooke (Electronics) and Glyn Beeby (Gearbox).

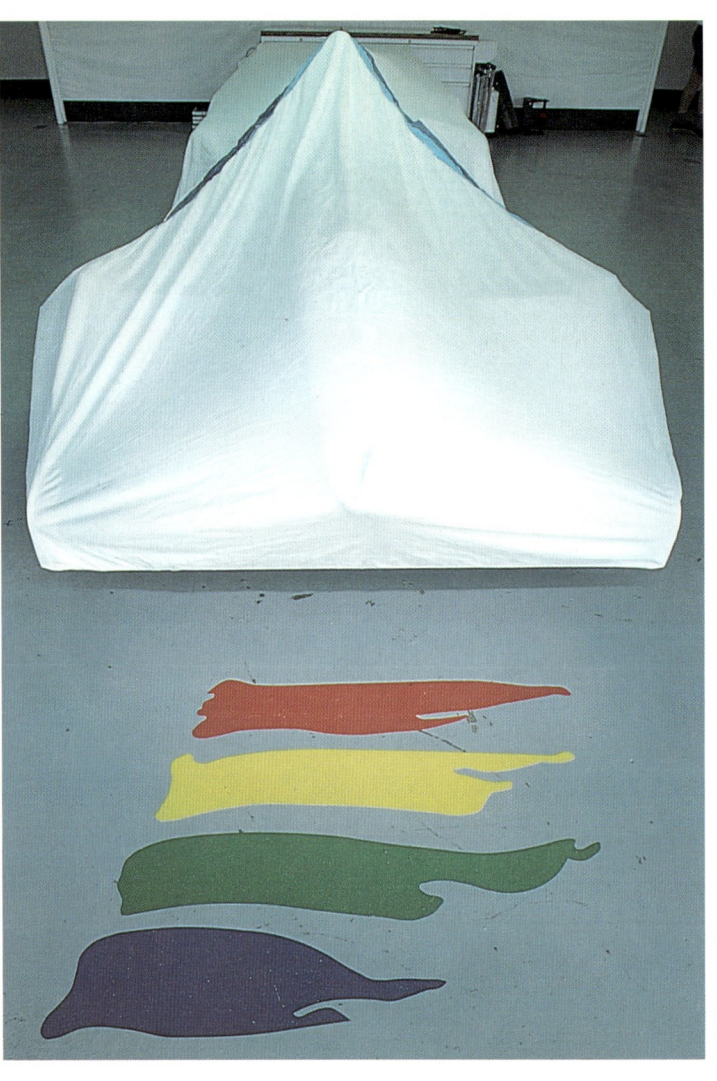

Thanks also to Patrizia Spinelli, John Postlethwaite, Rod Vicary, Jessica Salisbury, Charlotte Hare, Mary-Anne Beveridge, Jean Campiche and Gerald Sezille of TAG Heuer. Barry Griffin and his Goodyear team, Martin Whitaker, Luigi and Ada Montanini, Victoria Hayter and Dave Morgan.

Special thanks also to Alistair Watkins and Pat Behar of the FIA for 'smoothing the way' at the races, and to Matt Mayo of Kodak, Simon Coleman and Jakki Moores of Nikon UK, Tim Haskell of KJP and to Ed Davis and Paul Cox of Sky Photographic, London. And lastly my thanks to Ruth Binney of Studio Editions for believing in the project and to John Lee and Paul Effeny for putting it together.

Chris Bennett, November 1995